John Wesley said: "What we need is a desire to know the whole will of God, with a fixed resolution to do it. Brondon says on page 119; "We discern the will of God by pursuing the heart of God." This book is about the pursuit of God. So, we track our progress in prayer by becoming" fixed." The Psalmist says; My Heart is fixed O God; my heart is fixed." (Psa. 57:7) Only then we will begin to see the Kingdom of God manifest in our day and on our watch. I highly recommend, *When You Pray, Say...*

Scott Kelso, General Overseer –
5 Points Greater Columbus Apostolic Network,
Columbus Ohio

This book contains a message of hope regarding our father's plan to bring forth the return of His Son into the earth through encounter prayer. Since this book comes to us from a godly man of prayer, I urge you to read it carefully and prayerfully

Bob Sorge, author, bobsorge.com

This important book, directing our focus on encountering Christ in prayer to transform our hearts and hasten his return, will inspire and help anyone who reads it.

Mike Bickle
International House of Prayer, Kansas City

When You Pray Say

WHEN YOU PRAY SAY

7 Prayers of Encounter to transform hearts and regions to Hasten the Return of The Lord

BRONDON MATHIS

When You Pray, Say – 7 Prayers of Encounter to transform hearts, regions and hasten the return of the Lord.

Copyright c 2019 *by Brondon Mathis*

All Rights reserved

Unless otherwise noted, all Scripture quotations are from the King James Version of the Bible. Copyright 1979, 1980, 1982 by Thomas Nelson, Inc, publishers. Used by permission.

Scripture quotations marked NIV are from the Holy Bible, New International Version. Copyright 1973, 1978, 1984, International Bible Society. Used Permission

Cover design by *Brondon Mathis*

ISBN 9781979299305

Printed in the United States of America

Table of Contents

FOREWARD……………………………………………………………………7

PREFACE - Understanding the High Priestly Prayer of Jesus Christ – The Real Lord's Prayer………………………………………9

P A R T 1 – ENCOUNTER PRAYER & PROCLAMATION

INTRODUCTION - Encountering God in the Lord's Prayer…..19

1. The Power of a Corporate Prayer Gathering…………………25

2. 24/7 Prayer and Worship for City-Wide transformation……………………………………………………………43

3. When you Pray, Say……………………………………………………51

4. The Three Times A Year of Regional Corporate Prayer for Encounter in Scripture: *Passover, Pentecost, Tabernacles*……………………………………………………………65

P A R T 2 – PRAYING THE DISCIPLES PRAYER IN PHRASES IN THE SPIRIT

5. Praying through the Disciples Prayer to Answer the Lord's Prayer……………………………………………………73

6. *Our Father in Heaven*………………………………………………77

7. *Hallowed Be Thy Name*..**89**

8. *Thy Kingdom Come Thy Will be Done in Earth as it is in Heaven*..**103**

9. *Give us this day our daily Bread*...**119**

10. *Forgive us our Debts as we Forgive our Debtors*..**131**

11. *Lead us not into Temptation but deliver us from Evil*...**149**

12. *Yours is the Kingdom, the Power and Glory forever Amen*..**167**

P A R T 3 - MAKE US ONE – JOHN 17 UNITY & CITY FATHERS

13. The Process to John 17 Unity...**177**

14. The Revelation of Jesus Christ – *The Glory Encounter Needed for John 17 Unity* **187**

FOREWORD

Brondon Mathis served on staff at the *International House of Prayer* from 2009 to 2012. And I'm so glad for the years he poured into this movement of day and night prayer in the spirit of the tabernacle of David in Kansas City. And because Ohio is so critical to what God is doing in our nation and in the earth, I'm also glad to see what's going on in Columbus Ohio through prayer, worship and evangelism. Prayer is so essential to preparing cities for the Lord's return back into the earth. In Kansas City, we're praying for God to cover the earth with prayer before His return. So, we're really behind what God is doing through *Hope for Columbus* and ministries like it.

This book, directing our focus in prayer on encountering Christ to transform our hearts and our regions, is very important, because some prayers get answered really quick, but many prayers for a city, state or nation, you've got to measure those prayers by years and decades. So, to not get discouraged with prayer, our focus must be on encountering the beauty of Christ in prayer, not just on our stuff, or what we desire from Him.

I believe this book will inspire and help anyone who reads it, to get our focus in prayer back on where it should be – Him, while at the same time contending in joyful expectation for righteousness and justice to be established in our cities in the earth.

Mike Bickle,
International House of Prayer of Kansas City.

When You Pray Say

PREFEACE

UNDERSTANDING THE HIGH PRIESTLY PRAYER OF JESUS CHRIST
— The REAL Lord's Prayer — John 17

In August of 2015, Shiloh Christian Center in Columbus Ohio, *Pastor Johnny Amos*, was the host church for a 10-day 24-hour Solemn Assembly prayer meeting with many pastors and leaders from around the city and state coming together for non-stop continuous worship, prayer and evangelism, called **Hope for Columbus**. The Lord had moved upon Pastor Amos, Connie Tucker (of *Father Heart ministries)* and I, at different times and in separate places, that God wanted to bring our city together around worship, prayer and evangelism in the summer of 2015. After months of confirmation, divine connections, preparation and the Spirits' gathering in our region, our city came together to seek God in prayer for 10 days. During this Solemn Assembly we prayed for our city to be a *City of Hope, a Good City, a Strong City and a City of Refuge,* where businesses and the economy of our city would flourish, even if others around us didn't. During these 10 days we saw hundreds of people ministered to about the saving knowledge of Jesus Christ, healed and set free from addictions to drugs and sexual perversion. After these 10 days, later in 2015 and into 2016, 2017, major corporations, like Amazon distribution center, and the IKEA Home store, parts of Google and Facebook, all announced that they would be moving, either their corporate stores or major departments of their staff or distribution centers to Columbus, bringing thousands of Jobs into our city.

In 2016, as a result of the Hope for Columbus solemn assembly and a subsequent Statehouse public prayer vigil, I was invited to speak at the Sunday morning kickoff service at the Republican National Convention in Cleveland Ohio, and subsequently I was invited to the White House in 2017. All of this as a result of a 10-day 24-hour solemn assembly prayer gathering in Columbus Ohio, in 2015.

After these 10 days many were released by the Holy Spirit to go forth throughout our city to begin opening up prayer rooms from this Solemn assembly at Shiloh Christian Center, where prayer, worship and evangelism solemn assemblies were established for city-wide transformation. From these 10 days of Hope for Columbus at Shiloh it became our mandate to go throughout the city and throughout the nations to key churches in designated regions to establish gate-keeping churches that will host Solemn assemblies of prayer in their own sanctuaries, consisting of worship, prayer and evangelism in designated, at-risk communities and dark regions throughout the city, nation and world.

The Birthing of a Vision

Initially, I had received this vision, to combine prayer, worship and evangelism for city-wide transformation, 10 years earlier as director of Evangelism at World Harvest Church, Pastor Rod Parsley. As director of Evangelism, our team established and operated World Harvest Church's urban ministry, called *Metro Harvest Church – an outreach church comprised of four satellite community Hope Centers on each side of town.* These Hope Centers ministered to thousands in the urban areas of Columbus Ohio, through tent revival services, food programs, social and civic evangelism, job fairs, health fairs, and economic empowerment classes. Within a five-year period, over 10,000 people were impacted by the message of the gospel and trained to enter the work force from welfare through this urban outreach church. Subsequently we worked with the Mayor and the Chief of Police to curtail crime in these at-risk communities through the power of prayer, mass evangelism, and social action.

A Need for John 17 Unity

During this solemn assembly in the summer of 2015, in an effort to bring the Body of Christ from throughout the City together to accomplish this vision, I was impressed upon by the Holy Spirit to meditate, pray and share from John 17 for the unity of the body of Christ in Columbus Ohio. My heart and mind was directed specially to verses 22 and 23.

...that they may be one even as we are one. I in them and you in me, that they may become perfectly one, so that the world may know that you sent me and loved them even as you loved me.

John 17 is the high priestly prayer of Jesus Christ, set in the context of His imminent return to the glory He had with the father in heaven before the world began. This prayer is significant to these times we live in today, as the church comes down the stretch run approaching the end of the age and the return of Christ. This is Jesus' prayer for His disciples, and it details what He desires for His church as she approaches the difficult times that will come upon her in the world in the last days. It is significant to understand that one of His main prayer emphases' during these difficult times is that we would not be taken out of the world during these difficult times, but that we would be kept from the evil one. This is a theme also found in the prayer He taught His disciples to pray in Matthew 6:10. The disciples Prayer Jesus taught His disciples to pray in Matthew 6 answers His own Prayer in John 17

Mat 6:11 Lead us not into temptation but deliver us from evil.

Joh 17:15 I pray not that thou should take them out of the world, but that thou should keep them from the evil.

As a matter of fact, the prayer in Matthew 6 that He taught His disciples to pray, and the prayer in John 17 that Jesus Himself prayed, are tied together at every main point and in every phrase, as you will see throughout this book. One answers the prayer of the other.

God's Protection for His Body in Regions of Refuge – Solemn Assemblies of Prayer

In my book, *Building Cities of Refuge*, I share an encounter I had at the Call Prayer Assembly in Detroit in 2011, where God spoke to me in the midst of a 24-hour stadium prayer meeting in Ford Field, the Detroit Lions home field. God spoke to my heart and said;

"*Sacred Assemblies, like this 24hr CALL/DETROIT, are going to be God's prescribed method, to either avert the judgment completely, or lessen it in a geographical region, or prepare a generation to stand without offense in the midst of the economic, environmental, and military crisis that are clearly seen in Joel and passages that clearly articulate the conditions of the end of the age right before the Rapture of His people.*"

Joel 2:15 <u>Blow the trumpet in Zion; consecrate a fast; call a solemn assembly; 16 gather the people. Consecrate the congregation;</u> assemble the elders; gather the children, even nursing infants. Let *the bridegroom leave his room, and the bride her chamber. 17 Between the vestibule and the altar* **let the priests, the ministers of the LORD, weep and say, "Spare your people, O LORD**, *and make not your heritage a reproach, a byword among the nations. Why should they say among the peoples, 'Where is their God?'"* In order for the church to come together in solemn assemblies in any city for times of prayer and worship in times of trouble and shaking, we are going to need to understand Jesus' prayer in John 17 and we're going to have to understand how to pray the disciple's prayer in Matthew 6:10; Luke 11:1-13, corporately, for one another, with one another. These two prayers, one prayed by Jesus, and one prayed by those that call themselves disciples of Jesus, are connected together to fulfill God's will in the earth. One is prayed by Jesus for His disciples, that they would know the Father and His love, and for His disciples to be one with one another, as He is one with the Father in heaven. The other, the disciple's prayer, is prayed by His disciples, taught by Jesus, to answer His prayer for His disciples to know the Love, preservation and oneness that will be needed to endure the temptations coming at the end of the age. This book will teach you how to pray corporately, what this generation calls the LORD'S prayer in Matthew 6:10 and Luke 11:1-13, in order to answer Jesus' prayer for us to be one in John 17. You will also learn what Jesus was after when He prayed in John 17 – *for His disciples to encounter the Glory of God in Christ,* and how to receive your own encounter with Christ, as was revealed to John in the book of the Revelation of Jesus Christ. I don't believe it's a coincidence that the one disciple that records this high priestly prayer of Jesus for His disciples to see the Glory that He had with the father before the world was, is the one disciple that had an encounter with Him on the isle of Patmos, and records the most extensive revelation of the glorified Christ in scripture, called the book of *THE REVELATION OF JESUS CHRIST*.

In this prayer in John 17 we see what's on Jesus' heart for His disciples and what we should be focused on as we seek to fulfil His heart's desire here in the earth as committed Disciples of Christ. As the church embarks upon the most trying times of this age, understanding Jesus' high priestly prayer in John 17 and seeking to live it out in our families, communities of faith and in our cities, will become more and more necessary. John 17 is the most comprehensive view of what Jesus is presently praying for us seated at the right hand of the father. John 17 is what we should be pursuing in prayer the closer we get to the end of the age, as we are praying the prayer Jesus taught us to pray from Matthew 6:10; Luke 11:1-13. John 17 is the hope of Christs' heart, the hope for his people and the hope for our Cities. John 17 is the prayer that Jesus prayed before His death, burial and resurrection, but is the least recognized prayer of the prayers Jesus prayed while on the earth. But it's the most detailed description of any prayer Jesus prayed while on the earth. Most of the body of Christ over the last 500 or more years has highlighted and emphasized the prayer in Matthew 6:10 to the exclusion of His prayer in John 17, and we've only taught Matthew 6:10 as a prayer recital. Most people know and can recite this prayer, but very few are experiencing the life of Christ behind this prayer. However, they can SAY; *Our Father which are in Heaven, hallowed be thy Name, Thy kingdom come. Thy will be done in earth, as it is in heaven. 11 Give us this day our daily bread. 12 And forgive us our debts, as we forgive our debtors. 13 And lead us not into temptation but deliver us from evil: For thine is the kingdom, and the power, and the glory, forever. Amen.*

In this book you will go from just *saying* this prayer, to *PRAYING* this prayer, to encounter the revelation and life of Christ behind the prayer. We've called Matthew 6 *the Lord's Prayer* as if it's a prayer that Jesus prayed. However, upon closer examination, while this prayer in Matthew 6:10 is a prayer for His disciples to pray, it's not the prayer Jesus prayed FOR His disciples. It's not the *Lord's Prayer*. It's the prayer Jesus taught His disciples to pray for themselves. This prayer should more appropriately be entitled the *Disciples Prayer,* not the *Lord's Prayer*. Jesus would not pray this prayer, because this prayer involves being forgiven of sins. Jesus neither sinned, nor needed forgiveness for sins. John 17 should actually be called *the Lord's Prayer*. Because this is the prayer Jesus actually prayed, as the Lord of Glory, for his disciples. Secondly, I realized if we actually meditated on and memorized this prayer of Jesus in John 17 as we have the disciples' prayer in Matthew 6, we would understand better how to pray and why we pray the prayer Jesus taught us to pray in Matthew 6. We would also be closer to what He desires for us as the expression of a community of faith in unity in our world, more than we are today. Today our churches and communities of faith are so divided and splintered and look more like social clubs, or political parties than the *ecclesia* of God, called to bring God's government, based on love of God and love of one another, to the earth. They look more like us, than they do like Jesus. They look more like the world, than they do like *the book of Acts church*. Could that be because we've neglected Jesus' prayer for His disciples for so many generations? Once I realized that we should be giving as much attention to John 17 as we do to Matthew 6, I began meditating on, memorizing and praying Jesus' prayer in John 17 to be able to recite it like I was taught to concerning Matthew 6. As I did, I began to get understanding of both prayers, and the power and process to John 17 Unity as we prayed Matthew 6, together in our cities, and in our communities of faith, with the leaders of communities of faith all coming together in one place in the region.

A 10 Day Solemn Assembly for A United City Church for Regional Transformation – The Hope for the Nations

For 10 days I led hundreds of believers, with their leaders, in prayer for John 17 unity to transpire in our city. I felt like the Spirit of God was saying, this is the only *Hope for Columbus*, and for the cities of the earth. The more I prayed from John 17 for unity in the body of Christ in our city, the more I realized and received revelation of the power and process of the disciple's prayer in Matthew 6 being prayed together, corporately, to bring about the unity that Jesus prayed for His disciples in His high priestly prayer.

I felt that if I really looked to apply this prayer in John 17 to my heart and mind, God would open up to me the power and the process of Matthew 6, for communities of faith and whole cities to encounter the glory of John 17, to walk in supernatural unity and love....*FOR YOURS IS THE KINGDOM THE POWER AND GLORY FOREVER, AMEN.*

PART 1

ENCOUNTER PRAYER AND PROCLAMATION

INTRODUCTION

ENCOUNTERING GOD IN THE LORD'S (DISCIPLES) PRAYER

In 2017, two years after the 10 days of prayer, worship and evangelism at Shiloh Christian Center, we were still praying worshipping and evangelizing the region, day and night. What began as a 10 day solemn assembly turned into an ongoing day and night house of prayer at Shiloh. One night as I was praying in the night, I had a dream concerning how to pray, what is commonly known as *The Lord's Prayer*, to encounter God and build a culture of encounter prayer in God's house. I dreamed I was by myself in *the Hope for Columbus* prayer room, a 24/7 prayer room our ministry established in 2015, praying what's called, "*The Lord's Prayer in Luke 11:2; Matt 6:10,*" (*It's actually, the Disciples Prayer*). In the dream I was praying through the Lord's (Disciples) Prayer in phrases (7 phrases), saying the phrases from the prayer and then praying those phrases in tongues (*Praying in the Holy Ghost*), until I encountered the spirit and revelation behind each phrase. As I was praying the *Disciples prayer* in this manner, the room began to fill up with people coming to encounter God.

You've Been SAYING the Lord's Prayer but Now I'm going to Teach You How to Start PRAYING the Lord's Prayer

I believe this dream was a key revealed, as a way God wants to build encounter, Joyful prayer in His house of prayer – *Systematic*

Meditative Prayer through the 7 phrases of the LORD'S (DISCIPLES) PRAYER. When I woke from the dream He said, "*You've been SAYING the Lord's Prayer but I'm going to teach you how to start PRAYING the Lord's Prayer. Your generation has been saying this prayer, but they have not been praying this prayer, and consequently they have not encountered Me in order to bring heaven to earth.*

In this dream I had, *God said to me, I'm going build prayer in my body before I return, so that my body will know how to call heaven to earth.* In essence He was revealing to me how to pray through this prayer to hasten the return of the Lord. It was evident the urgency of God's heart concerning this prayer, that God wants to build us up in our prayer life, teaching us how to pray until He returns to set up His kingdom in the earth.

This is the only thing the disciples asked Jesus to teach them to do...*Lord, Teach Us to Pray.* This prayer teaching is a template of entrance into God's mind, for how He accesses our hearts to release His will into the earth, and how WE access heaven to bring heaven to earth.

The Seven Phrases of the Disciples Prayer

This prayer template revealed in the dream was broken up into 7 *PHRASES/DIMENSIONS IN PRAYER, ACCESSING 3 REALMS.* Those three realms are; 1.) The Heavenly realm, 2.) The Kingdom of God realm, and 3.) The Earthly realm.

Luke 11:1 It happened that while Jesus was praying in a certain place, after He finished, one of His disciples said to Him, **"LORD, TEACH US TO PRAY just as John also taught his disciples. 2. And He said unto them, "When you pray, say….**

1. *Our Father in Heaven" – The Heavenly realm of the Father's dimension in prayer*
2. Hallowed be thy Name – *The Heavenly realm of the Son's dimension in prayer*
3. Thy Kingdom Come Thy will be done in earth, as it is in Heaven – *The Kingdom realm of the Holy Spirit's dimension in prayer*
4. Give us this day our daily bread – *The earthly realm of the Word's dimension in Prayer*
5. Forgive us our Debts as we Forgive our Debtors – *The earthly realm of Man's dimension in prayer.*
6. Lead us not into Temptation but Deliver us from Evil – *The kingdom realm of the deliverance dimension in prayer.*
7. For yours is the kingdom, the Power and Glory forever Amen – *The Heavenly and Earthly realm convergence of the Worship dimension in Prayer.*

A Seven Day Weekly Prayer Format

Notice there are 7 phrases/dimensions of the Lord's prayer for each day of a 7-day week. In addition, notice the phrases of the 7 dimensions in prayer in Matt 6:10-14 begin with the **Father, the Son, and the Holy Ghost** (*thy kingdom come - the Kingdom of God is….in the Holy Ghost. Ro 14:17*), then it goes on to the **Word of God's dimension in prayer** (*Give us this day our daily Bread*), then onto **Man dimension's in prayer dealing with how to stay connected with God and one another** (*forgive us our debts as we forgive our debtors*). Then it goes on to **the deliverance dimension in prayer** (*Deliver us from evil*) and culminating in **the Worship dimension** in prayer (*for Yours is the Kingdom the power and the glory*). With there being 7 phrases/dimensions to this prayer for the 7-day week, this prayer can be prayed with an emphasis being placed on one of the phrases from this prayer for each day, in order to encounter the God behind each phrase weekly, monthly, yearly, until we bring heaven to earth.

The week begins with;

1. **The Father**...Our Father – (SUNDAY)
2. **The Son**...Hallowed be thy Name – (MONDAY)
3. **The Holy Ghost**...Thy kingdom come thy will be done in earth as it is heaven (the Kingdom of God is....in the Holy Ghost. Ro 14:17) – (TUESDAY)
4. **The Word of God/Supernatural provision**...Give us this day our daily Bread – (WEDSNESDAY)
5. **Reconciliation to God and one another**...Forgive us our debts, as we forgive our debtors – (THURSDAY)
6. **Deliverance from Evil**...Lead us not into temptation but deliver us from evil. – (FRIDAY)
7. **Our Worship dimension**...For yours is the Kingdom the power and the glory. – (SATURDAY)

In this dream I had in the prayer room in my city, I was sitting, praying The Lord's prayer with just a few people in the room. All the sudden the prayer room began to fill up. I turned to ask certain ones if they wanted to do worship, and before they could respond and go up, all these worship leaders began stepping up to sing and worship the Lord in a rotation. I turned and saw some of the leaders of the prayer room heading up to fix the microphones as I also went to help adjust the microphones, so the worship leaders that was suddenly coming to lead worship could be heard.

As I was leaving the building, the building was full of people standing, worshipping. And as I looked back there was a full band of African Americans singers and musicians that were standing behind their microphones/stands set up at the back of the church, facing the platform. They looked like they were ready to sing but the backs up of the people were facing the front also, so no one saw them. I walk to my left heading out the door facing them and motioned to one of the singers on the microphones to take down their stands and equipment. He motioned for me to get out of the way, not knowing what I was saying, nor who I was. I went forcefully towards him, as he cowered down, I whispered something in his ear. We then went to the back board that had the schedule on it as I was telling them that they can only set up to sing up front on the platform, not in the back.

What stands out most about this dream is how God began to fill the room with worshippers and singers, until the room was completely full. It was as I was praying through the *Disciples Prayer* that the room began to fill with those eager to encounter God and be healed and delivered in the presence of God.

The Disciples Prayer is to be Prayed Corporately...*With One Another, for One Another*

Next, what was impressed upon my heart from being in this prayer room with a microphone in my hand, sitting in the fourth row, was that I was being given a corporate imperative of this prayer. This prayer is a corporate prayer. Meaning, that it was meant to be prayed corporately, *with one another, for one another.* The prayer does not say *MY father*, but **OUR Father**...It does not say "*Give Me* this day *My* daily bread, but **Give US** this day **OUR** daily bread....It does not say, "*Lead Me not into temptation,*" but "**Lead US** not into"....It does say, "*Deliver Me from evil,*" but "**Deliver US** from evil."

I Began to Receive Divine Encounters with the God behind Each Phrase

In the dream as I was saying the phrases and then praying in tongues over each phrase, the Lord began to encounter my heart with the revelation behind each phrase of this prayer, until as I prayed the phrase OUR FATHER WHICH IS IN HEAVEN, I was standing in heaven before the father. For the phrase HALLOWED BE THY NAME, I began receiving a revelation of the SON, and our sonship inheritance in Him, until I was standing before the throne encountering the Son. For the phrase, THY KINGDOM COME THY WILL BE DONE IN EARTH AS IT IS IN HEAVEN, I was escorted from heaven to earth with a revelation of the Kingdom of Heaven, to bring heaven to earth through the power of the Holy Ghost, and on and on, praying in the Holy Ghost over each phrase of the disciples prayer until I received a revelation of that phrase, bringing me into an encounter with what I was saying and praying.

I woke up transformed from this dream. Even though I was dreaming, it was if I had been praying it in reality. And I immediately realized that we must start Praying this prayer, not just saying or reciting this prayer.

In this book you will learn how to spend time each day praying in tongues for 30 minutes and Meditating on a phrase from the disciples' prayer for 30 minutes to encounter God, His will and His plan for our lives, in calling His kingdom from Heaven to Earth.

In this book you will also receive a Holy Ghost focused prayer format to teach you how to focus on a phrase a day from the Disciples Prayer, for whole regions to be able to systematically pray together through this prayer Jesus taught His disciples to pray, to encounter God and bring heaven to earth.

CHAPTER 1

THE POWER OF A CORPORATE PRAYER GATHERING

It was 7:15 in the morning in Columbus Ohio as I was driving into what was normally nominal traffic on back country roads coming from a morning corporate prayer meeting that I frequented every morning at 5am. However, this morning as I was headed home from this early morning prayer meeting to get dressed for the day, the traffic was backed up unusually on this back road. As I slowly moved up the road, I could see that the reason for the traffic was not early morning rush hour, but a bad accident between a truck and a car.

As I came upon the accident the police were diverting the traffic from the accident to turn around and go back. Not wanting to go all the way back the other way, I motioned to the police if I could go around the accident through the grass on the side of the road. He gave me, and only me, access to go through the grass, as if I was a dignitary, turning everyone after me around to go down another road. As I drove through the grass, around the accident I could see that it was a head-on collision between the car and the truck. At that moment, I heard someone call my name from the midst of the accident. They had recognized my car and called out to me to come and pray for one of the victims. They were two women who had also been in the early morning prayer meeting. They were from the outreach ministry I had been heading up at the ministry I was a staff Pastor at. The young man in the accident was one of their disciples they had been caring for from the inner-city where we had been reaching out to.

He was a new believer, newly saved at one of our outreaches a few months before. He had been driving the car that slammed into the truck. He was 15 years old and had taken his moms car joy riding. And now he had been pronounced dead on the scene. As I pulled off into the grass and got out of the car the two ladies from the prayer meeting greeted me before I got to the car that had been demolished. They said, "It's Paris," "It's Paris" from the outreach last month. We ran over to the car as they were putting his body into the ambulance, and the MT's said, he's dead, as they shut the door to the ambulance. I looked through the window of the ambulance and could see they had placed him under the sheets. At that moment as the Ambulance was pulling off, I heard the Holy Ghost say, "Follow that Ambulance to the Hospital" *"He's not dead but sleeping."* **Wake Him up!** I Immediately got in my car and followed the ambulance to children's hospital. All the way to the Hospital I kept saying Awake, Awake Paris! Wake UP, Wake UP! You're not Dead. Wake UP! Awake, Awake Paris, *Put on your strength.* (Isa 52:1)

When I arrived at the hospital I was met by his Mom and her drug dealing boyfriend. As she approached me crying, I said to them, HE'S NOT DEAD! They said, they just told us he was dead. I said again, HE'S NOT DEAD. HE'S ASLEEP. Then I said to them, If God brings him back, will you surrender your lives to Him? Through tears they said, YES! YES! I said, lets pray a prayer of surrender, surrendering your lives to the Lordship of Jesus Christ, and then let's pray for your son, to wake up. They then repeated after me as I led them in a prayer of surrender and then commanded her son to wake up, declaring AWAKE, AWAKE PARIS, PUT ON THY STRENGTH!!! As we finished praying, the door opened to a room in the back where they placed the bodies for autopsies. The doctor, excitedly exclaimed, HE'S AWAKE...HE JUST WOKE UP...And there's nothing wrong with him but a bruise on his head. No broken bones and no other injuries. He can be released with aspirin for his headache. The mother and her boyfriend thanked us, hugged us and committed to join us in our outreach ministry, leading young teens and young adults to Christ. From that miracle of that young boy being raised from the dead, subsequently over the next six weeks over 6000 young people were saved at the ministry that I was staff Pastor and Outreach director, as we had ongoing services calling young people to Jesus Christ.

The Power of a Corporate Prayer Meeting

As I was driving home from the hospital that day, there were two questions on my heart that I began dialoging with the Lord about, between thanking Him, and praising Him for the miracle of the boy raised from the dead. Firstly, *what just happened? What Just Happened Lord?* He was dead, and now he's alive without a broken bone in his body, with a car mangled beyond recognition or repair?

The second question, was "Why don't miracles of the dead being raised and powerful signs and wonders, drawing many to Christ, happen more often in our region or in our Christian culture? And to these two questions the Lord began asking me a series of questions that I had not considered. He said, *"where were you coming from as you drove up on that accident?"* I thought, and then I said, I was coming from a prayer meeting at 5am in the morning. We had been leading early morning prayer for a few years, associated with the outreach ministry I was directing, with 50 to 100 people coming and praying each morning, and at its peak we had seen up to 800 people coming to pray and cry out for God to save our city at 5 am every morning Monday through Friday. After this the Spirit of God began asking me a serious of questions about miracles that happened in the early church in the book of Acts.

- QUESTION #1: Where were disciples on the day of Pentecost coming from when 3000 souls where added to them?

  ANSWER: *The Upper Room gathering of 120 in prayer waiting on the power from on High. Acts 1:12-2:41*

- QUESTION #2: Where were Peter and John headed when they came upon the lame man at the gate beautiful and said, "Look on us" …. silver and gold, have I none…. rise and walk…and 5000 were added to the church?"

  ANSWER: *They were headed to the temple at the ninth hour, at the hour of prayer. Acts 3:1*

- QUESTION #3: Where had the disciples just come from when in Acts 5… At the hands of the apostles many signs and wonders were taking place among the people Insomuch that they brought forth the sick into the streets, and laid them on beds and couches, that at the least the shadow of Peter passing by might overshadow some of them….and even more believers in the Lord, multitudes of men and women were constantly added to their number?

  ANSWER: *They had just come from the Acts 4 prayer meeting where they had gathered together, and the place was shaken, and they were all filled with the Holy Spirit and Began to speak the word of God with boldness…and the multitude of them that believed were of one heart and of one soul: neither said any of them that ought of the things* which he possessed was his own; but they had all things common. And with great power gave the apostles witness of the resurrection of the Lord Jesus: and great grace was upon them all. Act 4:31-33*

- QUESTION #4: Where had Stephen come from when in Acts 6 it was reported, *And Stephen full of grace and power, was performing great wonders and signs among the people?*

  ANSWER: He had just come from the prayer meeting with the Apostles over the increasing in the widows being overlooked in the daily serving of food, where when they chose seven men of good report and full of the spirit and wisdom….and after praying they laid their hands on them and the word of God kept on spreading and number of the disciples continued to increase greatly in Jerusalem. Act 6:1-7

- QUESTION #5: Where did Phillip come from in Acts 8, before he went down to the city of Samaria and began proclaiming Christ to them…and many who had unclean spirits were coming out of them shouting with a loud voice and many who had been paralyzed and lame were healed?

  ANSWER: He had just come from the same prayer meeting with the Apostles in Acts 6 where when they chose the seven men of good report and full of the spirit and wisdom…and after praying they laid their hands on them and the word of God kept on spreading and number of the disciples continued to increase greatly. Acts 6:1-7

- QUESTION #6: What took place in Acts 8 with Peter and John before all of Samaria received the Holy Spirit?

> *ANSWER: The Apostles heard in Jerusalem that Samaria had received the word of God, and they sent Peter and John to have a prayer meeting for them to receive the Holy Spirit. And in verse 14 Peter and John prayed for all of them that they might receive the Holy Spirit and then began laying their hands on them and they all received the Holy Spirit. Acts 8:14-17*

This went on and on, up until Acts 16, with God asking me questions of how miracles of healings, salvations and deliverances took place in the book of Acts, directly connected to a corporate or small group prayer, praise or worship encounter with Christ, that resulted in manifested power and demonstration of the Holy Ghost.

Corporate prayer and miracles go hand in hand. But most of our prayer teaching within the body of Christ is focused only on individual prayer time. Therefore, we have little, if any teaching or biblical organizing around corporate prayer. In this book with this prayer format from the disciple's prayer you will learn and understand the importance of corporate prayer, and in Chapter 4 you will learn how corporate prayer in a congregational setting was done in scripture. This prayer format from the disciple's prayer is a corporate prayer initiative with a focus on both individual and corporate prayer for divine encounters with both power and glory.

How to Organize Corporate Intercession in the House of God

And when they had prayed, the place where they were assembled together was shaken; and they were all filled with the Holy Spirit, and they spoke the word of God with boldness." (Acts 4:24-31)

What is corporate intercession? Corporate Intercession is intimate partnership and agreement with God and man for His purposes to be established in the earth.

1. Intercession is intimacy. Prayer is an exchange of romance. God speaks to us and it moves our hearts. When we speak back to God, His heart is moved. God desires to establish or deepen this romantic relationship with us. He desires intimacy with us. He wants us to know His heart and more so, to feel the very emotions of His heart, and then He wants to hear us cry out for the longings of His heart to come to pass. His longings become our longings. It's partnership at the most intimate level possible. In intercession, we begin to feel and do what God feels and does. *"For Zion's sake I WILL NOT HOLD MY PEACE, and for Jerusalem's sake I WILL NOT REST..." (Isaiah 62:1) "I have set watchmen on your walls, O Jerusalem; THEY SHALL NEVER HOLD THEIR PEACE day or night. You who make mention of the Lord, do not keep silent, and GIVE HIM NO REST..." (Isaiah 62:6)*

2. Intercession is partnership. Intercession is the means by which God's will is established on earth. God does not act apart from human beings partnering with His heart. Intercession expresses the bridal identity of the church. There is nothing more powerful that can fuel God's heart to move upon the earth than the cry of His bride, whose desires reflect His own.

3. Intercession is agreement with God. Intercession is agreement with what God promised to do. When we ask God to do what He desires to do, we are declaring that we agree that His desires are good, and that His desires have become our desires.

Intercession Expresses God's Definition of the Church

"...My house shall be called a HOUSE OF PRAYER for all nations." (Isaiah 56:7)

"...PRAYER ALSO WILL BE MADE FOR HIM (JESUS) CONTINUALLY, and daily He shall be praised." (Psalm 72:15)

"PRAY WITHOUT CEASING..." (1 Thessalonians 5:17)

What Do I Do During an Intercession Set?

Experience enjoyable prayer. *Experiencing God's beauty and God's burning desire for us is what makes prayer enjoyable.* Experiencing God's beauty and desire is the primary source of power that will fuel the end-time prayer movement. The power to engage in night and day prayer is found in having a heart that enjoys God. Encountering God's beauty and desire for us is where we most enjoy our primary reward, which is God Himself. Our primary reward is not the breakthrough of revival. Revival is fantastic, but it is our secondary reward. Jesus Himself is our primary reward. We carry this reward inside our hearts. In other words, we live with a fascinated heart as we drink deeply of God's beauty and desire for us.

Experience God's Beauty - This means to understand and experience revelation of the attributes of God as given by the Holy Spirit. This leads to an elation of our spirit, which can be felt in our emotions and which transforms the way that we think and feel about God, ourselves and others.

Experience God's Desire - This means to understand and sense, or feel, what God wants to do in us, in others and in the events of human history on the earth and into eternity. When the Holy Spirit reveals this information to us, we can actually feel the emotions of God's heart inside of us. It is an exhilarating sensation that energizes and frees us from wrong mindsets.

How Do We Experience God's Desire?

Praying the prayers of Scripture. Prayer that comes from God's heart expresses His desires. This is the kind of prayer that the Holy Spirit releases Divine authority on.
This is the kind of prayer that God answers. Praying the prayers that come from God's heart enhances the enjoyment of our intimacy with Jesus. The Disciples prayer, or Apostolic prayers are prayers that the apostles prayed. The chief apostle is Jesus, and the 12 apostles have prayers recorded in the New Testament. These apostolic prayers are God's very prayers, or desires.

Practice Praying Positive Prayers*:* When we pray positive prayers, we enter into the delight of asking for the things that bring pleasure to God. This is a gateway into feeling His desire in our inner man. New Testament Biblical prayers focus on releasing God's grace instead of hindering or removing negative realities like sin or demons. There is a positive focus on the impartation of good instead of a negative focus on removing the realities of sin. The New Testament focus usually flows along themes of joy, thankfulness and victory.

* We do incorporate the negative dimensions of prayer that target confessing, resisting and renouncing the realities of the world, flesh and devil. However, we recognize that they are not the major focus of the New Testament model of praying.

Practical tips for Praying Positive Prayers:

Pray to God instead of talking to people when you pray corporately. Focus on "asking" "*receiving*" and-or *declaring* instead of "explaining. "Speak directly to God – be more conscious that He is watching and listening than that others are watching and listening. This will prompt you to direct your heart toward *Him* in love and partnership. Lift specific promises of Scripture up to God and ask for their fulfillment in our present-day context.

Ask for the in-breaking of positive things rather than the removal of negative things. Example: Positive Prayer: *"Father, I ask that Your light and truth would break in upon the church in this City!"* Negative Prayer: *"Father, I ask that You remove darkness and deception from the church this City!" *Note: God hears, cares about and discerns all prayer, whether positive or negative. Because of our natural human tendency to become weary and discouraged, praying positive prayer allows us to maintain prayer day in and day out by helping us engage in joyful supplication rather than trying to bear the emotional weight of negative realities expressed through negative prayer. This is especially relevant in a 24-7 prayer ministry. It is because of both the Biblical model and human dynamics that we encourage positive prayer.*

Prayer on the Microphone

Everyone is welcomed and encouraged to pray on the microphone. Praying on the microphone is in no way mandated but encouraged as a way to engage your heart in intercession and to help lead the prayer meeting. Anyone can do this, no matter what their personality, style, or disposition.

A Few Helpful Tips for Praying on the Microphone

a. If you wish to pray on the microphone, make your way to the front row. They will fill up quickly. Be prepared to wait at least 45 minutes for your turn since the prayer meeting is intermingled with worship and other prayer focuses.

b. Select a New Testament prayer or Old Testament prophetic decree to pray out of. The "key apostolic prayers" list is a great place to start.

c. Please hold the microphone VERY close to your mouth (to prevent sound feedback in the room). Don't feel any pressure to shout on the microphone, rather speak at a moderate volume level.

d. You have the option to pray with the singers or not. If you pause, the singers on the platform will begin singing spontaneous prayers. Within every 2-3 short songs, you may interject more short prayerful phases. In this way, we are going back and forth in team ministry in intercession.

e. Pray "positive prayers." (See *"practical tips for praying positive prayer,"*)

f. When you are finished, feel free to simply set the microphone down and walk away.

How to Pray Using the Apostolic Prayers or Old Testament Prophetic Decrees in the Harp and Bowl Model:

a. Decide what or who the target of your prayer is examples: The church in Columbus Ohio, the church in any city or nation, the government of a country, the loss of any city or nation, etc.

b. Using the "Disciples Prayer Phrase" List or "Prophetic Decrees and Promises from OT Prophets" Pick the prayer phrase or decree that best expresses what you want to pray for.

Example #1: If you want to pray that the church in your city would encounter power you could announce; "I'm praying The Disciples Prayer phrase, *"Thy Kingdom Come Thy Will Be Done in Earth as It Is In Heaven"* From Acts 1:6-8. Then, read it out loud so everyone knows the scripture focus; Act 1:6 When *they therefore were come together, they asked of him, saying, Lord, will you at this time restore again the kingdom to Israel? 7 And he said unto them, It is not for you to know the times or the seasons, which the Father hath* *put in his own power. 8 <u>BUT YE SHALL RECEIVE POWER, after that the Holy Ghost is come upon you</u>: and ye shall be witnesses unto me both in Jerusalem, and in all Judaea, and in Samaria, and unto the uttermost part of the earth.* Then begin praying for the church in your city to receive a power encounter like they did on the day of Pentecost.

Example # 2 Or if you want to pray that the church in your city would grow in the knowledge of Jesus, you might pick an *Apostolic Prayer from Ephesians 1:17 to read aloud; "THAT THE GOD OF OUR LORD JESUS CHRIST, THE FATHER OF GLORY MAY GIVE TO YOU THE SPIRIT OF WISDOM AND REVELATION IN THE KNOWLEDGE OF HIM, the eyes of your understanding being enlightened, that you may know what is the hope of His calling, what are the riches of the glory of His inheritance in the saints, and what is the exceeding greatness of His power toward us who believe, according to the working of His mighty power." (Ephesians 1:17-19)* Then begin praying for the spirit of revelation to come up the church in your city, etc, etc. in Jesus Name.

Example #3: If you want to pray that the church in your city would experience revival, you might pick the *Prophetic Promise* found in Isaiah 35:1-2: *"The wilderness and the wasteland shall be glad for them, and THE DESERT SHALL REJOICE AND BLOSSOM AS THE ROSE; IT SHALL BLOSSOMABUNDANTLY AND REJOICE, EVEN WITH JOY AND SINGING..." (Isaiah 35:1-2)*

1. No matter what you want to pray for, you should be able to find an Apostolic Prayer scripture or choose a Disciples prayer phrase or a Prophetic promise to match the cry of your heart – they cover pretty much everything. Feel free to ask the associate prayer leader to help you find an Apostolic Prayer or Prophetic promise that matches the burden of your heart.

2. It's okay if you don't feel anything "burning" in your heart. If you don't feel something specific that you want to pray for, just pick any prayer phrase from the disciple's prayer or a promise – all of these prayers and promises are on God's heart all of the time, so it's impossible to pray the wrong prayer!

3. You can choose to pray through just a phrase or a section of the Apostolic Prayer or Prophetic promise. You don't have to pray through the whole prayer/promise.

If helpful, create an outline of the prayer from your meditation you receive as you're praying in the spirit. This may help you to organize your thoughts and therefore present a clear train of thought for others to follow as you lead the room in intercession. Pick 2-3 points (actual phrases from the Apostolic/Disciples Prayer or Prophetic promise) to pray through. Your prayer will be more focused if you concentrate on a few points of the prayer, rather than trying to pray through all of the points and themes of the prayer.

4. Make notes under each of your main points as you prepare to pray. Include cross-references and your own expression of the Biblical prayer or promise.

5. Pray through each of your points, one at a time, either pausing to let the singers sing or not. Practice articulating your heart.

Why Is It Important to Articulate Our Hearts?

It is exhilarating to develop language to express the truth that God deposits in our hearts through His Word. We feel the sensation of pleasure in our heart when we express God's truth through our own understanding and with our own vocabulary. Human Beings are the only creatures on earth who are given the gift of language.

It is an awesome and fascinating privilege to be able to communicate the depths of our heart to each other and to God. By developing an ability to put the ideas and feelings that are in our hearts into words, we do a couple of things:

- We explore the emotions of God's heart more deeply.
- We inspire others to identify stirrings in their hearts.
- We expand our own understanding of the Word of God.

How to Articulate Your Heart

Practice putting passages of Scripture into your own words. Example: *"That the eyes of your understanding would be enlightened." "That the innermost part of your spirit would be illuminated" "That your innermost man would be awakened by the light of God" "That the eyes of your heart would fully comprehend"*

Cross-referencing is another wonderful tool – finding other Bible verses that explain or expound upon your point to articulate yourself. How good it is to use the Bible to expound on the Bible! It may be helpful to use a thesaurus to expand your vocabulary when meditating on the apostolic prayers.

How to Lead Others in Intercession

When you pray on the microphone, you are helping to *lead* a prayer meeting. When prayer leading or praying on the microphone, the goal is to *serve* the room. The following are Values that are important to remember when praying on the microphone:

1. Team ministry – we go farther together;

2. Inclusiveness – everyone can participate;

3. The centrality of the Scripture – God's language unifies our heart with His and others.

The following are some dynamics to keep in mind when you are praying on the microphone.

1. Volume – Though it is necessary to hold the microphone very close to your mouth and to speak clearly, *there is no need to shout on the microphone*. A moderate volume level is encouraged, with an occasional projection or shouting volume. The room is not engaged by continual shouting, but rather by dramatic contrasts. Theologically, shouting does not mean that we are more gripped with the Holy Spirit or that we are making a greater impact in the spiritual realm. Authority is not manifested by volume, but by Divine activity.

2. Clarity – This means that it is clear to the room what your prayer focus. Your main points are clearly defined and prayed through and they follow each other in a logical way. Repeating key phrases and using concise statements creates clarity.

3. Topic – Is your prayer focus one that the majority will be eager excited to partner with you on? Praying for the church in your city…., or the government of our nation, etc., are examples of focal points that the majority can join with you in. Praying for a friend or relative that no one knows except you may cause disinterest and disengagement of others. Again, we pray on the microphone to lead and serve the room in Intercession. Praying on the microphone does not make our prayer any more important to God; rather, it is a tool that helps us join together in prayer.

4. Enthusiasm – Are you passionate about your prayer? Does it show? Others will be more inclined to join in with your prayer if they sense that your heart is engaged and burning.

This does not mean shouting or exaggerating your emotions. This means being aware that you are being heard by others and that you are trying to bring them along with you in intercession. Monotone speech or a casual delivery may cause others to disengage. Remember that you are speaking to God —connect with Him and your passion will be expressed.

5. Length of Prayer – 5 minutes is a pretty good length. If you go longer than 5-7 minutes, often the room will lose interest and disengage. Also, there are usually others waiting to pray after you.

6. Timing– You may want to add little 2-3 second phrases *in between* the singers' singing – not during their singing – to reiterate your point to the room. *Please do not shout over the choruses.* Also, it is helpful to read the room in terms of when to begin warring in the spirit. Usually it is best to go into a time of warring in the spirit when the music and the singers are the most intense sounding.

There are more dynamics to be aware of when praying on the microphone, but these are the main ones. It will take time to learn to lead the room, but the more you go up there and pray, the more you will learn, the easier it will become and the more enjoyable it will be.

Rapid Fire Prayer

What is rapid fire prayer? Rapid Fire Prayer is a series of short prayers, prayed on the microphone one after the other, interspersed by choruses from the prophetic singers.

Why do we do it? Rapid Fire Prayer provides an opportunity for more people to pray on the microphone per intercession set and it also can bring energy to a prayer meeting because of the energizing dynamic of the short "bursts of prayer" from several different voices. How does a rapid-fire prayer cycle work? The prayer leader will announce a rapid-fire cycle. He or she will announce what the prayer focus is and will invite 10 – 15 people (anyone who wants to) to come up and *pray a ten to fifteen second prayer* on the microphone. The Rapid-Fire cycle leader will start by praying a one- or two-minute prayer. After that prayer, the singers will sing a chorus. Then one by one, those in line will pray a ten to fifteen second prayer. In between every few intercessors' prayers, the singers will sing a chorus. Then, the next person will pray and so on until everyone in line has prayed. Rapid fire prayer is a great way to begin praying on the microphone if you are nervous or just want to get a "feel" for it.

The Corporateness of Prayer

Most believers don't understand the importance of corporate prayer - *that your individual prayer time is for your corporate prayer time* (Matthew 6:6)..*But you, when you pray, enter into thy closet, and when you have shut the door, <u>pray to your Father</u> which is in secret*. If you don't have an individual prayer time you won't have an inflow of power to flow into you, and your corporate prayer time won't have the greater power of agreement when the body comes together. And if you have don't have a corporate prayer time you won't have an outlet to release of power to flow into the world. So not only should you have an individual prayer time, but you should have a corporate prayer time with a body of believers (Matthew 6:9)...*After this manner therefore pray ye: <u>Our Father</u> which art in heaven...* Jesus stated this prayer format in such a way that it would be most effective when prayer was made individually and corporately - *for one another, with one another*, to release miracles signs and wonders into the earth.

CHAPTER 2

24/7 PRAYER AND WORSHIP FOR CITY-WIDE TRANSFORMATION

LORD, remember David and all his afflictions – Ps.132:1-8

In scripture whenever Israel went astray, God raised up spiritual reformers with a vision to restore worship, as a young man turned king in the bible named David, commanded it, to enquire of the Lord in His temple, to behold the beauty of the Lord. As a young man, in his teens - 20's, David made a vow to dedicate his life to find a resting place or dwelling place for God. This refers to a place where an unusual measure of God's presence is manifest on earth. David's life work was to establish a dwelling place for God in Jerusalem in his generation.

1 LORD, remember David and all his afflictions; 2 How he swore to the LORD, and vowed to the Mighty One: 3 "Surely I will not go into the chamber of my house, or go up to the comfort of my bed; 4 I will not give sleep to my eyes...5 until I find a place for the LORD, a dwelling place for the Mighty One of Jacob"...8 Arise, O, Lord, to Your resting place (Ps. 132:1-8). David vowed to live in extravagant devotion to seek the Lord with all his resources (time, talents, treasures). His vow included spending time in God's House (Ps. 27:4), fasting (Ps. 69:7-12), extravagant giving of his money (1 Chr. 22:14) and embracing God's order in worship. This vow changed history and continues today in those who embrace it. It is at the heart of the End-Time worship movement. I believe the Lord will raise up a million believers who fully walk out this vow. David's vow positioned his heart to receive insight into the worship that God seeks.

23 True worshipers will worship the Father in spirit and truth; for the Father is seeking such to worship Him. (Jn. 4:23)

David received revelation of worship in God's heavenly sanctuary (1 Chr. 28:11-19).

96 I have seen the consummation of all perfection (God's Throne of Glory) ... (Ps. 119:96.) 11. David gave his son Solomon the plans...12 for all that he had by the Spirit, of the courts of the house of the LORD...13 also for the division of the priests and the Levites, for all the work of the service of the house of the LORD...19 All this," said David, "the LORD made me understand in writing, by His hand upon me, all the works of these plans." (1 Chr. 28:11-19)

2 I heard a voice from heaven, like the voice of many waters, and...loud thunder. I heard the sound of harpists...3 They sang...a new song before the Throne... (Rev. 14:2-3)

Just like in the biblical history of the communities of God's people Israel, when they went astray, God raised up reformers who restored worship as David commanded. God, in the earth in this generation, is going to raise up reformers who will restore worship once again as David commanded, to worship, sing and pray, until whole cultures in communities are changed. As I stated in my preface earlier, I believe the strategy for bringing forth Justice and communities that are righteous, is day and night prayer and worship with singing in the spirit of the tabernacle of David.

The KJV version of the bible says that God "inhabits (lives in or manifests His life) in the praise or songs of His people. David taught that when we sing praise that God inhabits (manifests His power) in that context.

3. You are...enthroned (manifest the power of Your Throne) in the praises of Israel. (Ps. 22:3)

David's revelation of heavenly worship (as seen in Psalms) is foundational to David's throne which is "political government in the spirit of the Tabernacle of David" or government based on 24/7 worship and intercession. David's government flowed forth from prophetic worship (1 Chr. 23-25). David had revelation of the spiritual impact of prophetic intercessory worship (Ps. 22:3).

6 Let the high praises of God be in their mouth... 7 to execute vengeance (justice) on the nations, and punishments on the peoples; 8 to bind their kings with chains...9 to execute on them the written judgment-- this honor have all His saints. (Ps. 149:6-9)

All the 7 "Old Testament revivals" restored this. Solomon established the singers according to the direction that God gave his father David.

> *According to the order of David his father, he (Solomon) appointed...Levites for their duties to praise...as the duty of each day required...for so David...commanded. (2 Chr. 8:12-14)*

Josiah's revival (about 625 BC) restored full-time singers and musicians as David commanded. Jehoshaphat and Jehoiada restored worship in the order of David (2 Chr. 20:19-28; 23:16-18).

> *He said to the Levites...4 "Prepare yourselves...following the instruction of David..." 15 The singers...were in their places, according to the command of David... (2 Chr. 35:3-15) J. Zerubbabel established full-time singers and musicians as commanded by David (Ezra 3:10-11). Ezra and Nehemiah established full-time singers and musicians as David commanded.*

> *The Levites...give thanks...according to the command of David...45 The singers and the gatekeepers kept the charge of God...according to the command of David... (Neh. 12:24, 45)*

> *In the days of Zerubbabel and Nehemiah all Israel gave the portions for singers... (Neh. 12:47)*

A Call to 24/7 worship with Prayer in this Present Generation

In May 1983, the Lord called the International House of Prayer in Kansas City (ihopkc.org) to establish the first 24/7 House of prayer with singing and worship in the spirit of the Tabernacle of David in the United States. In 1999 they actually launched out in this call. As a result, many Houses of Prayer have begun popping up all over this nation and the world since that time as a prophetic sign at the end of the age of the preparation for the return of the Lord. But there are very few of these places of day and night worship and singing with prayer in the African American communities. Which is strange considering our gifts and talents in the areas of the arts, singing, and in dance. Therefore, because our communities are not participating in this 24/7 worship, singing and prayer phenomenon happening all over the world, our communities are lacking righteousness and justice. The definition of the word "Justice" means to be conformed to righteousness. It's not until our communities are conformed to righteousness that we will see the Justice of God released into our communities. Psalm 89:13 says God's throne is established on the foundation of righteousness and justice. *Psa. 89:14 Righteousness and justice are the foundation of your throne; steadfast love and faithfulness go before you.*

My Introduction to 24/7 Prayer at IHOPKC

In April 2008 I visited this place of 24/7 worship, singing and prayer called I.H.O.P for the first time. When I got there, it was 3:00am in the morning and the place was full of young people singing, dancing rapping and praying to the Lord in the session they call, *The Night-Watch*, which goes from 12 midnight to 6am in the morning. This got my attention immediately, as I saw a 24hr format of prayer and worship lining up with the 24/7 Wal-Mart grocery stores of the 21st century. What I saw at IHOP lined up perfectly with the business trend of this age, with 24-hour 7 day a week business, television stations, gas stations and grocery stores. It also lined up with a dream I had in 1999 of worshippers and those gifted and talented in the arts coming into my father's little store front church in Columbus Ohio, lined up miles down the road waiting to get in to that building to worship, sing and dance, day and night. I was stunned when I found out that I.H.O.P.K.C began in 1999 when God first had me close down my father's church for what was coming in the 21st century. WOW! To say I was flabbergasted was a major understatement.

I was totally captivated that weekend by everything. The Spirit of God had spoken to me and told me back in 1999 that His church will not be able to keep up with this generation, with the evil being proliferated by the forces of darkness in this generation, with a Sunday only approach to Christianity, while the culture is a non-stop 24/7 culture. The first Century church in scripture was not a Sunday morning Christian expression of Christianity, but a daily, house to house, temple prayer expression (Acts 2:46,47).

Act 2:46 And they, continuing daily with one accord in the temple, and breaking bread from house to house, did eat their meat with gladness and singleness of heart, 47 Praising God, and having favor with all the people. And the Lord added to the church daily such as should be saved.

Embracing David's Revelation of Worship in the Old Testament

> *11 On that day I will raise up the Tabernacle of David, which has fallen down, and repair its damages; I will raise up its ruins, and rebuild it as in the days of old... (Amos 9:11)*

Jesus requires night and day prayer as the condition to release justice. Prayer is a very practical expression of the commandment to love one another in that it releases deliverance for the needy. The revelation of intercession affected David's method of government. He established 24/7 worship and intercession as the foundation of his kingly reign in Israel (1 Chr. 23-25). His revelation of heavenly worship (as seen in Psalms) is foundational to David's throne which is "political government in the spirit of the Tabernacle of David" or government based on 24/7 prophetic worship and intercession. He had revelation of the power of worship (Ps. 22:3).

> *3 You are holy, enthroned (release power) in the praises (singing the Word) of Israel. (Ps. 22:3) 6 Let*

the high praises of God be in their mouth... 7 to execute vengeance (justice) on the nations, and punishments on the peoples; 8 to bind their kings with chains...9 to execute on them the written judgment-- this honor have all His saints. (Ps. 149:6)

HOPE FOR COLUMBUS – 24/7 Worship Prayer & Evangelism for City-Wide Transformation

In the summer of August 2015 HFC launched the vision to conduct 10 days of 24hr prayer, worship and evangelism at Shiloh Christian Center at 787 E. Broad St. in Downtown Columbus, the center of the city, to pray for our city and our nation's racial, and political climates. We saw many salvations, healings, and deliverances, with many now being discipled at Shiloh. Since this mighty move of God, we have been released by the Holy Spirit to unite as many churches as possible to Shiloh Christian Center, to bring Hope to Columbus, by raising up a city-wide 24/7 prayer room in the center of the city. And from Hope for Columbus at Shiloh it is our mandate to go forth throughout the city to the churches of Columbus to conduct 3, 7, or 10, days of non-stop 24-hour prayer, worship, and evangelism, to ignite the fires on the altar of our city. We will look to the Holy Spirit to identify 12 key gatekeeping ministries on each side town to raise up these regional Hope Centers for City-Wide revival and regional transformation.

Hope for Columbus is a vision and strategy to call the body of Christ in our city to city-wide solemn assemblies of prayer, worship and evangelism. It is a vision to ignite the fires of revival and release the Christ within the Hope of Glory, to transform our city and region for God. These Solemn assemblies will consist of 24/7 worship, prayer and evangelism in a centralized location and subsequent locations throughout the city for open heavens over the region to release city-wide transformation.

The 21st century strategy for these prayer and benevolent outreaches would be adapted to follow God's end-time pattern of day and night solemn assemblies, beginning in a central location in the city, to begin raising up 24/7 Prayer, Worship and Evangelism centers of Hope (Hope Centers) throughout the city. Out of the initial solemn assembly in a central location, HFC would begin targeting 4 inner-city neighborhoods to host 10-day 24hr solemn assemblies of prayer, worship and evangelism, each culminating in 3-day tent revival services in the designated neighborhood. These services on each side of town will be followed up by raising up of ongoing 24/7 Houses of Prayer and Worship Missions bases in the region where the tent services have operated. During these HFC outreaches we will seek to rally whole neighborhoods and communities, as well as the City-Wide Body of Christ to a Stadium gathering of worship and prayer for our city on a designated date, followed by quarterly or yearly stadium solemn assemblies of Prayer and worship. This will begin restoring within these communities and our city, the Love for God and our neighbor.

Through prayer and the discipleship ministry of Jesus Christ we will invade the communities of this city, rebuilding the old waste places and raising up the foundations of many generations, giving hope for the hopeless, and help for the helpless, putting the Neighbor back in the Hood, *Saying what God says to us when we encounter Him in Prayer.*

CHAPTER 3

WHEN YOU PRAY, SAY...

The Biblical Theology of Holy Spirit Empowered Corporate Prayer Meetings

Act 4:31 And when <u>they had prayed</u>, the place was shaken where they were assembled together; and <u>they were all filled with the Holy Ghost,</u> and <u>they spake the word of God</u> with boldness.

Prayer is a spiritual activity where we access heaven or the spirit realm to bring what is unseen of the spirit realm into earth, or into the natural realm. The spirit world is accessed by words. John 6:63 says, *"The words I speak, they are Spirit and they are life."* The Spirit world is accessed by words. This is why Jesus said; *When You Pray, say...* Entering the spirit world or the heavenly realm requires both praying and saying. Prayer is communication with God to line up what we say with what He's saying, to produce His will in the earth, as it is in Heaven. Words are how we communicate or establish His will in the earth realm. *Prayer is how we get the right words to Say.* So, to connect the earthly realm with the heavenly, and the heavenly realm with the earthly realm it requires **Praying** and **Saying**.

And He said unto them, "When you pray, say…Luke 11:2

1Co 14:12 Even so ye, forasmuch as ye are zealous of spiritual gifts, seek that ye may **excel to the edifying of the church**.

1Co 14:13 Wherefore let him that speaks in an unknown tongue **pray that he may interpret**.

1Co 14:14 **For if I pray in an unknown tongue, my spirit prays**, *but my understanding is unfruitful.*

1Co 14:15 What is it then? **I will pray with the spirit, and I will pray with the understanding also:** *I will sing with the spirit, and I will sing with the understanding also.*

In the dream, I was sitting in the chair and I was saying phrases from the first through the seventh realms of the disciple's prayer and then *PRAYING IN THE HOLY GHOST (TONGUES),* over each phrase of this prayer, from the *Father's dimension of prayer* through to *the deliverance dimension in prayer* on unto the *worship dimensions of prayer - Yours is the kingdom the power and the glory.*

After each phrase I would begin praying in tongues. As I would pray in tongues, after saying each phrase of the prayer, I began getting a revelation of the phrase I was saying. For example: The first phrase is; *"Our Father which are in Heaven."* Then as I began praying in tongues, I began getting a revelation of the Father's heart, as well as a revelation of Heaven, and what's going on in heaven around the throne. In this prayer room I began to encounter God in a corporate setting. The fact that I had a microphone in my hand, sitting in the fourth row, was an indication to me that I was being given a corporate imperative to pray this prayer in a corporate setting. This prayer, The *LORDS/Disciples prayer*, is a corporate prayer format. Meaning, that it was meant to be prayed corporately, *with one another, for one another*. The prayer does not say *MY father*, but **OUR Father**...It does not say "*Give Me* this day *My* daily bread, but **Give US** this day **OUR** daily bread"....It does not say, "*Lead Me not into temptation*," but "**Lead US** *not into*"....It does not say, "*Deliver Me from evil*," but "***Deliver US*** *from evil*."

As stated earlier, most believers don't understand this very important point about the duality of our mandate to pray, both the individuality and corporateness of prayer - that you should have both an individual prayer time (Matthew 6:6)..*But you, when you pray, enter into thy closet, and when you have shut the door, <u>pray to your Father</u> which is in secret*...and you should have a corporate prayer time with a body of believers (Matthew 6:9)...*After this manner therefore pray ye: <u>Our Father</u> which art in heaven*... Jesus stated this prayer format in such a way that it would be most effective when prayer was made individually and corporately - *for one another, with one another*.

Secondly, this prayer was meant to be prayed in the spirit, by the power of the Holy Ghost. Most believers don't understand this teaching to involve praying in the Spirit. Therefore, we don't receive from God, who is a Spirit *(God is Spirit...John 4:24)*, when we pray the *Disciples Prayer* in Matthew 6:10; Luke 11:2-13.

You Receive the Holy Ghost to Receive from God in Prayer

If you then, being evil, know how to give good gifts to your children, how much more will your heavenly Father <u>give the Holy Spirit to those who ask Him</u>?" (Luke 11:13 NASB)

One of the overlooked parts of the teaching on prayer from both Luke's and Matthew's version of Jesus' teaching on prayer is that Jesus connects asking in prayer with receiving the Holy Ghost in both versions. In Matthew 7:7-11 and Luke 11:13, He closes out the teaching on prayer stressing the need to receive the Holy Ghost in prayer when you ask, knock and seek the Father in prayer. It's also worth noting that He compares a good father in the natural as one that he gives good things to his children, with our Heavenly being no different. Our heavenly Father also gives good things to His children. But His way of giving is through the giving of the Holy Spirit. Father God is a spirit and to receive from a God which is spirit you must access the realm of the spirit through the power of the Holy Ghost. If God were flesh, access to receiving from Him would be the works of the flesh. But because He is not flesh, the access to receiving from Him is the workings of the Holy Ghost.

Luke 11:9 Tells us how to begin the process of receiving from God, saying; *Ask, and you shall receive, Seek and you shall find, Knock and the door will be opened...EVERYONE WHO ASKS AND CONTINUES TO ASK, RECEIVES.* But notice He doesn't give you what you ask for. In verse 13 is says, HE GIVES THE HOLY GHOST TO EVERYONE THAT ASKS. Why? because God is a Spirit, not flesh. YOU are the one with a body, but His body is His church. YOU are a Spirit that lives in a body. Therefore, to receive from God who is a Spirit, HIS BODY, the church, must receive the Holy Ghost for everything we ask for.

The Holy Ghost Is How God Fathers Us.

He gives the Holy Ghost for whatever we ask for. The very fact that we ask God for anything is indicative of the fact that God is *OUR FATHER*. The fact the we have received the Holy Ghost is indicative of the fact the GOD IS FATHERING US. Ask and keep on Asking, seek and keep on seeking, knock and keep on knocking and HE WILL CONTINUE TO GIVE THE HOLY GHOST TO EVERYONE THAT ASKS.

How do You Pray in the Spirit?

When I speak of receiving the Holy Ghost for those things you are asking for, I'm referring to receiving the spirit's unction to pray in the Spirit. There are two ways to pray in the spirit. One is through praying in tongues, and the other is through praying the Word of God. The bible says in John 6:63, it is the Spirit who gives life; the flesh profits nothing; *the words that I have spoken to you are spirit and are life.* Because the word of God is Spirit, praying or saying the word of God IS prayer in the spirit. However, praying the word of God without the spirit's leading is not productive. I do not advocate just going to the bible and looking up scriptures to speak over your carnal prayer requests. Unless the spirit is prompting you from the place of prayer there will be no power in your praying to produce what you're saying. Praying the Word of God without the spirit's leading is no more productive than complaining or murmuring in prayer like the children of Israel in the wilderness. They eventually received what they we're wanting but it sent leanness to their souls.

Psa. 106:13 They soon forgot his works; they waited not for his counsel: 14 But lusted exceedingly in the wilderness, and tempted God in the desert. 15 And he gave them their request; but sent leanness into their soul.

Praying in the Spirit begins with allowing the Spirit of God to lead us to the Word He's wanting us to SAY over our situation we have before Him. When we allow the spirit of God to lead us to the word of God to Say over our situation, we line up our words in earth with His words in Heaven. And when we do, we agree with God's report and establish His will in earth as it is in Heaven. This is how God created the heavens and the earth, He didn't just say, *"Let there be light."* Before He said anything over the Heavens and earth, *the Spirit of God first moved upon the face of the waters...And God SAID.*

*Gen 1:1 In the beginning God created the heaven and the earth.
2 And the earth was without form, and void; and darkness was upon the face of the deep.* **_And the Spirit of God moved upon the face of the waters. 3 And God said, Let there be light: and there was light._**

The Spirit of God moving upon the face of the waters, is the Spirit of God moving upon the words spoken with creative power. The Word of God in scripture is compared to water in Ephesians 5:22

Eph 5:26 That he might sanctify and cleanse it with the washing of water by the word,

The word spoken from the place of prayer in the spirit has creative power to release life to any situation that's dead, or that's anything less than what God said it would be in the beginning. When we PRAY and SAY, we release creative life.

Once you Pray in Tongues You must Say in English

To *Pray* is to speak to God and have God speak back to you His Word and will for your life in the earth. To *Say* is to speak from God, to man, or to speak to what belongs to man, what God just said to you when you prayed. In I Corinthians 14 Paul teaches on prayer, referring to *Praying* (in tongues) as *speaking unto God*. Many people debate in theological circles whether or not speaking in tongues is for everyone. My first question concerning that belief is a practical question from a theological and biblical perspective. My question would be; *In the New Covenant, does God only desire for some people to talk to Him, as in the First Covenant? Or is it God's desire for everyone to talk to Him?* If God desires for everyone to talk to Him, then it has to be God's will that everyone speaks in tongues, because 1 Cor 14:2 says, HE THAT SPEAKS IN AN UNKNOWN TONGUE SPEAKS TO GOD.

Paul's Teaching on Corporate Prayer to the Corinthian Church

Paul's teaching in I Cor. 14 is actually the most comprehensive teaching on corporate prayer in a congregational setting in all of scripture. Paul is teaching on prayer here, not the gifts of the spirit. Many theologians think Paul is teaching in I Corinthians 14:1 on the gifts of the Spirit, and specifically the *gift of divers tongues*, found in I Cor 12:10. However, Paul is not teaching on the gifts of the spirit in 1 Cor 14 he's teaching on *SPIRITUAL THINGS as related to how to PRAY corporately in the spirit to SAY in English what God told you to say when you prayed in the spirit*. Paul is teaching on prayer in a congregational setting. When to PRAY and when to SAY. Or when to pray in tongues and when to prophesy in the straight (native) tongue.

The word *"gifts"* in I Cor. 14:1 is italicized, meaning that it was added by the translators. It should actual read...*Follow after charity, and desire spiritual THINGS, but rather that ye may prophesy* (SAY). Paul is teaching I Cor 14, how and when to pray in both a personal, private setting and in a corporate, congregational setting, and what to focus on in prayer in both settings, how to receive from the spirit of God in prayer in both settings, in order to edify, encourage and comfort the congregation of the saints. The first thing Paul emphasizes about prayer in I Cor. 14, is that our ultimate desire should be to prophesy, or to SAY in prayer. Prayer is not complete with just *PRAYING* in Tongues. Prayer is not consummated until you're *SAYING* in English, or your native tongue. This means we are to desire to speak what God is saying from the spirit realm into the natural, earthly realm out of a corporate prayer time in the Holy Ghost.

Secondly, when Paul taught on spiritual things as related to prayer, in a both a personal and corporate setting, He taught that when we pray tongues we speak to God. 1 Co 14:2 *For he that <u>speaks in an unknown tongue</u> speaks not unto men, but unto God...*

Thirdly, when Paul taught on spiritual things, he taught that when we pray in tongues, we speak the mysteries of God, giving us the ability to know things about God and us that we cannot know without God revealing it to us. 1Co 14:2 *For he that speaks in an unknown tongue...speaks mysteries.*

Fourthly, Paul taught that when we *prophesy, we speak unto men for edification, and exhortation, and comfort.* The term "Men" is speaking in the plural, specifically speaking of a congregational setting. So in a congregational setting, we can all pray in tongues to speak to God corporately, as long as when we speak to God corporately in an unknown tongue, there's someone to interpret what we're saying, so HE can speak back to us, answers that comfort, edify and exhort us to build up the body on our most holy faith to bring the known will of God from heaven to earth.

1Co 14:5 I would that ye ALL spoke with tongues, but rather that ye prophesied: for greater is he that prophesies than he that speaks with tongues, except he interpret, that the church may receive edifying.

After this Paul also established what praying in tongues releases into a corporate expression of prayer. There are four main manifestations of speaking in tongues. Those four main purposes of speaking in an unknown tongue in a corporate setting are encountering God through (1) revelation, (2) knowledge, (3) prophesy, and through (4) teaching.

1Co 14:6 Now, brethren, if I come unto you speaking with tongues, what shall I profit you, except I shall speak to you either by revelation, or by knowledge, or by prophesying, or by doctrine?

So, our aim as we speak to God through prayer in the spirit should be to encounter God personally to prophesy, or speak to men publicly for edification, exhortation, and comfort. Therefore, Paul emphasizes in the first few verses of I Cor. 14 that we should speak to God through prayer in tongues (I Cor 14:2) to edify ourselves with God's mysteries concerning what we need to know that we are yet unaware of, until we know what He knows to speak to men in the earth. We should speak to the church to edify the body through prophecy, saying in our native tongue only after we have prayed in the spirit to build OURSELVES UP. We pray in the Spirit to build ourselves up. We say in our native tongue to build others up. So, we Pray (In tongues), to Say (Prophesy) in English or our native tongue.

Jud 1:20 But ye, beloved, building up yourselves on your most holy faith, praying in the Holy Ghost,

Praying-Saying in the Holy Ghost is for Witnessing His Kingdom in the Earth

Acts 1:5 for John baptized with water, but you will be baptized with the Holy Spirit not many days from now." So, when they had come together, they were asking Him, saying, "Lord, is it at this time YOU ARE RESTORING THE KINGDOM TO ISRAEL?" Acts 1:5-6 NASB

One purpose of the Holy Ghost to cause you to receive the mysteries of God's kingdom to cause you to walk in the truth of the teachings of the kingdom of God AS A WITNESS to what's coming in the earth when the King, YESHUA returns to rule and reign in righteousness. However, I want to bring to your attention that another main purpose of the Holy Ghost is to declare in prayer (prophesy), *THY KINGDOM COME THY WILL BE DONE IN EARTH AS IT IS IN HEAVEN.*

The purpose of the HOLY GHOST power is to talk about, preach about, pray and testify of the coming King and His coming Kingdom to the earth. And if you're not praying forth, talking about or preaching about the soon return of the King and His Kingdom back into the earth, you may not have the biblical expression of the Holy Ghost, but a religious, denominational expression. The power of the Holy Ghost is to prophecy or call heaven to earth...*saying COME LORD JESUS...The SPIRIT and the Bride say COME* (Rev 22:14). When the Disciples received the Holy Ghost in the Upper room Peter gave us the prophetic purpose of the Holy Ghost in Acts 2:17; *And it shall be in the last days God says, that I will pour forth of My spirit on all mankind and your sons and your daughters shall* **PROPHESY** *, and your young men shall SEE VISIONS , and your old men shall DREAM DREAMS* (Acts 2:17 NASB)

The prophetic purpose of the Holy Ghost is to prophesy about Jesus, to see visions of Jesus, to have dreams of Jesus, to be empowered to say, *"THY KINGDOM COME THY WILL BE DONE IN EARTH AS IT IS IN HEAVEN."*

If we're not calling heaven to earth, if we're not talking about the coming of the LORD, we might not have the power of the Holy Ghost as the bible says, to witness of Him, and His return to set up His Kingdom in the earth, first in Jerusalem and then to the uttermost parts of the earth. (Acts 1:6-8). I was awakened to the nearness of His return and our need to be prepared at the heart level, with the experience of the expiring of My Passport and me not knowing until we got to NYC in 2018 on our way to Jerusalem. He said if you're not continually preaching about or talking about MY return you will not be ready for MY return at the heart level. Then He reminded of what Matthew 7:22, 23 says;

22. Many say to me on that day, Lord, Lord, did not we prophesy in your name, but I will say DEPART FROM ME I NEVER KNEW YOU.

You will not be ready at the heart level (the Passport of your heart expired), because you received the Holy Ghost to preach, sing and do work for me, instead of to be near me to become like me, as a witness of my return.

Fasting Prepares you to Pray and Say with Power

The Spirit is preparing the Church for the greatest revival and the most intense pressure in human history. Radical changes are needed, but they will surely come. The Church will be prepared before Jesus returns (Rev. 19:7). What the Western church accepts as normal will change dramatically. How do we cooperate with the Spirit so that we may talk and walk in the intimacy and power that the New Testament church walked in? Part of the answer is to embrace the fasted lifestyle. This speaks of walking in the spirit of fasting in food, finances, and the use of our time, words, and energy. Many fears fasting but the fear of fasting is actually far worse than the fast itself.

Fasting is, by definition, abstaining from food. Fasting is part of the normal Christian life. It is often thought of as an optional discipline. Jesus said, "When you fast," implying that fasting occurred in the regular course of a disciple's life. 17"When you fast…*18 your Father who sees in secret will reward you openly."* (Mt. 6:17-18). Jesus called us to fast because He knows that its rewards will far outweigh its difficulties. With boldness, Jesus emphasized that the Father will reward fasting (Mt. 6:17). This proclamation alone makes fasting very important. God rewards fasting, yet these rewards are not earned by us. Some of the rewards are external, as our circumstances are touched by God's power. Some of our rewards are internal, as our hearts encounter Him in a new depth. We fast both to walk in more of God's power to change the world, and to encounter more of His heart to change our heart! The idea that fasting changes us internally is a new idea to some. Fasting results in tenderizing our hearts. When this occurs, we make different choices, which lead to different outcomes in the places we go and the people we meet. When our values are different, it affects who we marry, how we raise children, how we spend our money, and what focus we have in ministry. Fasting embraces voluntary weakness in order to experience more of God's power and presence. It is a paradox that we become weak in the natural in order to receive more strength from the Spirit. Jesus revealed to Paul that the release of God's power in his life was connected to his willingness to embrace weakness. This revelation is foundational to understanding the purpose of fasting. 9"My grace is sufficient for you, for My strength is made perfect in weakness." (2 Cor. 12:9)

Five different type of food fasts: 1. The regular fast is going without food and drinking only water or that which has no calories. 2. The liquid fast is going without solid food and drinking only light liquids (like fruit juices). 3. The partial fast, or Daniel fast, abstains from tasty foods and eats only vegetables or nuts, etc. 4. The Benedict Fast established by Saint Benedict (525 AD), consists of only one meal a day. 5. The absolute fast or Esther fast, abstains from food and water (Esth. 4:16). Exercise caution!

I urge most people to fast at least one day a week. Two days a week is better. It is a false notion that fasting is radical Christianity, and thus is optional to Christianity. Fasting is normal and basic to the Christian life. We are called to fast regularly. There are obvious exceptions. People who are pregnant or have health problems should consult their doctors before fasting.

Ministering the Baptism in the Holy Ghost

Step 1 Repent: First thing you need to do is repent:
Pray this prayer of repentance with Me:

Father in heaven, I'm coming to you asking you to forgive me of all my sins, hidden sin, secret sins, public sins, anything that's displeasing to you God, forgive me. Cleanse me by the blood of Jesus right now. Help me Lord to walk in victory, to walk in faith, to follow you, and to have deliverance in my life and heart today. I receive Jesus as Lord and Savior. Amen!

Step 2 Ask, Receive and Speak by Faith - You need to know 3 things to be baptized in the Holy Spirit.

1. *The same faith that you're saved with is the same faith you receive the Holy Spirit with.* You don't have to have a great faith, pray for faith, or pray more faith in. If you can believe what I'm saying you have FAITH.

2. *When you ask the Holy Spirit to come in…You have to ask him…*He will do what you ask Him if you believe.

3. *The Bible says, that when the Holy Spirit came on the day of Pentecost they spoke in tongues as the spirit gave them utterance….* And I like to say it this way. They spoke as the spirit gave them inspired words. - And when you are praying for the Holy Spirit to come in, you will at some moment hear the Holy Spirit speaking to you and it's your spirit praying…your spirit's receiving the power of God. And when you hear those words coming up in your spirit, speak it with your mouth and you'll feel the power of God being released.

Step 3 - Worship Him in Spirit and Truth - Worship in the Spirit (tongues) comes from knowing the truth about what God's word's saying about receiving the Holy Spirit through asking, seeking and knocking in faith. Let everyone that has their prayer language start worshipping in tongues and those that don't, start worshipping by faith in tongues.

Okay let's pray…pray this with me:

Heavenly father, according to your word, according to your promise. I receive the gift of the Holy Ghost right now. Spirit of God fill me, baptize me in God's power, with the Holy Spirit right now. I receive the Holy Spirt, now, right now, in Jesus name. Now lift your hands and start worshipping….

CHAPTER 4

THE THREE TIMES A YEAR OF REGIONAL CORPORATE PRAYER FOR ENCOUNTER IN SCRIPTURE:

Feast of Passover, Pentecost and Tabernacles

Without a return to the power of the spirit and a lifestyle of disciplined seeking of the Lord, through Prayer and fasting, both personally and corporately, we will never see the encounters and demonstrations of the spirit that the Acts church saw out of their 10-day Solemn Assembly in the upper room on the day of Pentecost. One of the reasons we don't have encounters with God in prayer is because we don't have regular corporate prayer times. Or if do have regular corporate prayer times, they are not kept during the seasons of divine encounter. Most Pentecostal believers don't realize that the 120 in the upper room were not just waiting for Christ to send back the Holy Ghost in Acts 1, but they were mainly waiting for the Day of Pentecost to come. Jesus sent them to wait for a divine encounter with the Holy Spirit during one of the three encounter times of the year in the Hebrew economy, the Feast of Pentecost.

Act 2:1 And when the day of Pentecost was fully come, they were all with one accord in one place.

Act 2:5 Now there were...in Jerusalem Jews, devout men from every nation under heaven.

Deu 16:16 Three times in a year shall all thy males appear before the LORD thy God in the place which he shall choose; in the feast of unleavened bread, and in the feast of weeks, and in the feast of tabernacles: and they shall not appear before the LORD empty:

*Lev 23:4 **These are the feasts of the LORD**, even holy convocations, which ye shall proclaim in their seasons. 5 In the fourteenth day of the first month at even is <u>the LORD'S Passover</u>. 8 But ye shall offer an offering made by fire unto the LORD seven days: <u>in the seventh day is an holy convocation:</u> ye shall do no servile work therein.*

The feasts of the Lord were times of encounter with the Lord, set into the Hebrew economy, where the children of Israel were to come together 3 times a year for holy convocations for 7 days with the Lord. During these feasts, set at the three times of harvest each year, they would bring a first fruits offering from their harvests unto the Lord. The New Testament Church of this generation has seemingly minimized the importance of understanding and keeping the feast observances in their seasons. Mostly because of Paul's admonition about not being bound to sabbath days, new moons and holydays. Colossians 2:16 *Let no man therefore judge you in meat, or in drink, or in respect of a holyday, or of the new moon, or of the sabbath days: 17 Which are a shadow of things to come; but the body is of Christ.*

But notice, Paul says, these days are a shadow of things to come, and the consummation of the shadow is the body of Christ. Because you have the body, that doesn't negate the calling to observe the seasons. It's just meant to focus you on encountering Christ, not the just the symbolisms and the shadows of what the ceremonial times were unto. Notice Paul's admonition in 1 Corinthians 5:8

*8. **Therefore let us keep the feast**, not with old leaven, neither with the leaven of malice and wickedness; **but with the unleavened bread of sincerity and truth.***

He does not tell them not to keep the feasts, but to keep the feast according to the truth, and with sincerity of heart. The feasts are built-in times of encounter with the Lord, solemn assemblies with the Lord to celebrate, commemorate and encounter, or meet with the Lord three times a year. During the times of Jesus' ministry, not only did Jesus keep the feasts, most of His miracles were done around the feasts. Especially in the gospel of John, the majority of the miracles that are recorded, Jesus was either going to the feast, at the feast or just leaving the feasts. This was because the feasts were the times, they were accustomed to gathering together for times of meeting with God, and Jesus being God, manifested himself at these times to reveal the father in the season when they were accustomed to encountering Him.

*Joh 2:23 Now when he was in Jerusalem **at the Passover Feast, many believed in his name when they saw the signs that he was doing.***

*Joh 4:45 So when he came to Galilee, the Galileans welcomed him, **having seen all that he had done in Jerusalem at the feast**. For they too had gone to the feast.*

*Joh 5:1 After this there was a feast of the Jews, **and Jesus went up to Jerusalem.***

*Joh 6:4 Now the Passover**, the feast of the Jews, was at hand. Joh 6:5 Lifting up his eyes, then, and seeing that a large crowd was coming toward him,** Jesus said to Philip, "Where are we to buy bread, so that these people may eat?" :6 **He said this to test him, for he himself knew what he would do.***

Joh 7:2 Now the Jews' Feast of Booths was at hand. *3 So his brothers said to him, "Leave here and go to Judea, that your disciples also may see the works you are doing.*

Joh 7:10 But after his brothers had gone up to the feast, **then he also went up, not publicly but in private.**

Joh 7:11 **The Jews were looking for him at the feast**, and saying, "Where is he?"

Joh 7:14 About **the middle of the feast Jesus went up into the temple and began teaching.**

Joh 7:37 **On the last day of the feast, the great day, Jesus stood up and cried out, "If anyone thirsts, let him come to me and drink.**

Joh 10:22 At that time the Feast of Dedication took place at Jerusalem. It was winter,

Joh 11:56 They were looking for Jesus and saying to one another as they stood in the temple, "What do you think? That he will not come to the feast at all?"

Joh 12:12 The next day the large crowd that had come to the feast heard that Jesus was coming to Jerusalem.

Joh 12:20 Now among those who went up to worship at the feast were some Greeks.

What if the body of Christ joined together as Jews and Messianic Jews in focused prayer for revival each season during *Passover, Pentecost and Tabernacles* until Jesus opened the gates, doors and heavens and released miracles signs, wonders, and divine encounters, along with the outpour of His spirit like the day of Pentecost? What if we gathered together in unity with expectancy in our hearts, convinced that God in His infinite wisdom and planning knew that this year at this time we would all be in unity? What if we did this while knowing that the Scriptures teach us that when we are in unity, walls shake and chains break? As you take the revelation and understanding you receive from this book, on the biblical calling to gather in seasonal corporate expressions of regional prayer and fasting, and begin calling solemn assemblies of corporate prayer, I look forward to hearing the testimonies of miracles from those who will choose to step out of their comfort zones and traditions and join together on these *Appointed Times*.

We need a hunger and thirst after God that cannot be filled by food and drink. We need a return to extended times of fasting and prayer that was originally seen in the gatherings of the Children of Israel three times a year, in Passover, Pentecost and Tabernacles in the Hebrew economy. We need divine encounters with the God we preach about. When we do, these times of encounter with God in the seasons of the feast will release regular times of Holy Ghost Baptisms and demonstrations of power and glory. We must seek these seasons of fresh baptisms as we come together in the times and seasons designated by God, to seek the Lord in corporate times of prayer and fasting.

Joe 2:15 Blow the trumpet in Zion; **consecrate a fast; call a solemn assembly;**

Joe 2:16 gather the people. **Consecrate the congregation; assemble the elders; gather the children, even nursing infants**. *Let the bridegroom leave his room, and the bride her chamber.*

Joe 2:17 Between the vestibule and the altar let the priests, the ministers of the LORD, weep and say, "Spare your people, O LORD, Joe 2:28 **"And it shall come to pass afterward,** *that I will pour out my Spirit on all flesh; your sons and your daughters shall prophesy,* *your old men shall dream dreams, and your young men shall see visions.*

Now that we understand the power of Holy Spirit inspired prayers with fasting, in the corporate setting, in the designated seasons of *Passover, Pentecost and Tabernacles*, I believe we're ready to enter into a 7-day, 7 phrases, prayer and fasting *Solemn Assembly* to encounter God and transform our regions. In the next section in we're going to walk through the *Disciples Prayer in phrases*, taking a phrase per day, praying in tongues over each phrase, and giving you a meditation for each prayer phrase for you to meditate on for each day, along with scriptures to meditate on for each day. I also want to suggest that as you meditate on a phrase each day from these 7 phrases of the *Disciples Prayer*, that you fast until 6 pm, pursuing after and seeking the face of God for the next 7 days.

PART 2

PRAYING THE DISCIPLES PRAYER IN PHRASES IN THE SPIRIT

CHAPTER 5

PRAYING THROUGH THE DISCIPLES PRAYER TO ANSWER THE LORD'S PRAYER

In order for the church to return to corporate solemn assemblies of prayer and worship as they did in the book of Acts, we are going to need to understand why He instructed His disciples in Matthew 6:10 to *pray in this manner*. It was to answer His prayer in John 17. Jesus' prayer in John 17 is actually connected to the prayer Jesus gave to His disciples to pray at every point. When we pray the disciple's prayer in Matthew 6 and Luke 11, we answer Jesus' prayer that He prayed in John 17. These two prayers, one prayed by Jesus, and one prayed by those that call themselves disciples of Jesus, are connected together to fulfill God's will in the earth. One is prayed by Jesus for His disciples, that they would know the Father and His love, and for His disciples to be one with one another, as He is one with the Father in heaven. The other, the disciple's prayer, is prayed by His followers to answer His prayer He prayed for them.

John 17 is one of the most significant prayers in the whole of scripture. Primarily because it was prayed by Jesus Himself before He returned to His glory He had with the father before the world began. It's also because it gives us a glimpse into what He's presently interceding for at the right hand of the father in Heaven. However, it is one of the most overlooked and least emphasized of all the biblical prayers in scripture. Yes, we lift verses from John 17 that highlight our need to be ONE in HIM as He is in Heaven, but we overlook the details and what it is He desires for His church as she approaches the difficult times that will come upon her in the world in the last days. As we understand what Jesus prayed for His disciples, we will have a greater understanding of the importance of praying through the disciple's prayer in phrases in the Holy Ghost, not just reciting this prayer religiously.

12 Things Jesus Prayed for us in John 17 - *The Lord's Prayer*

There are 12 points of emphasis in the prayer Jesus prayed for His disciples that we must know to get God's heart for His body. They are;

(1) *That we would understand (eternity) eternal life (v.2).*

(2) *And that in-understanding eternity we would come to a greater understanding (knowledge) of the father and the son (v.3).*

(3) *That we would understand the name of god (Jesus) that the son came to manifest in the earth (v.6).*

(4) *That we would receive and understand the words (messages) god gave Jesus to give to us (v.8).*

(5) *That we would be kept in the name of Jesus (v.11)*

(6) *That we may be one as he and the father are one (v.22).*

(7) *That we may have our joy full by the words (messages) god gave Jesus to give to us*

(8) *That we would be kept in the world, while being kept from the evil one (v.15)*

(9) *That we may sanctified (set apart from the world) in the truth of the word of god (v.17)*

(10) *That our calling and process of coming into unity in him (the body of Christ, racially, & nation/states) would be a part of the process of perfecting (maturing) us (v.23)*

(11) *That we would have encounters with the glorified Christ (that we may see his glory) (v.22).*

(12) *And that the love with which the father loved the son may be experienced by us, his disciples (that we would know the love of the father) (v.26).*

In this prayer in John 17 we see what's on Jesus' heart for His disciples and what we should be focused on as we seek to fulfil his heart's desire here in the earth as committed Disciples of Christ. John 17 is the most comprehensive view of what Jesus is praying for us seated at the right hand of the father. As we look to answer Jesus' Prayer that He's praying at the right hand of the father, we will release the answers to the prayers of the saints from the disciple's prayer in Matthew 6:10; Luke 11:2-13. And it is the prayer focus of these above points of emphasis from John 17 that we should be praying and pursuing the closer we get to the end of the age. It is the hope of Christs' heart, the hope of Glory, and the hope for his people, as well as the hope for our Cities. ***John 17 should be called the Lord's Prayer. Because this is the prayer Jesus actually prayed, as the Lord of Glory, for his disciples. Secondly, I realized if we actually meditated and even attempted to memorize this prayer of Jesus in John 17, as we have the disciples' prayer in Matthew 6, we would be closer to what He desires for us as the expression of a community of faith in our world than we are today.***

The First dimension into the Disciples Prayer

The first dimension into God's heart for praying through the Disciples/Lord's prayer in phrases is the Father dimension in prayer. The Father dimension in prayer is the doorway into the heavens, or the spirit realm. Our natural father's in the earth are supposed to connect us to our Heavenly Father in heaven. A natural father establishes our revelation of God as a father. This fatherhood dimension in prayer is a revelation of what the father looks like, acts like and how the father trains you for heavenly access. As I was saying and praying; *Our father which is in heaven*, I began getting a revelation of Father God, as well as my role as a father, responsible for leading disciples into a relationship with father God. I also began being healed of father wounds and things that I didn't get from my earthly father, that hindered me in my relationship with Father God. In that very moment God began giving me the responsibilities of an earthly father that prepares us to receive from God in prayer. This training for heavenly access can be seen in the context of the text of the teaching of the prayer he taught His disciples to pray. A father teaches reliance and dependence upon God and His kingdom. Mat 6:25 says. *Therefore, I say unto you, take no thought for your life, what ye shall eat, or what ye shall drink; nor yet for your body, what ye shall put on. Is not the life more than meat, and the body than raiment? 26 behold the fowls of the air: for they sow not, neither do they reap, nor gather into barns; yet your heavenly father feeds them. Are ye not much better than they? Mat 6:32 (for after all these things do the gentiles seek:) for your heavenly Father knows that ye have need of all these things. 33* **But seek ye first the kingdom of God, and his righteousness;** *and all these things shall be added unto you.*

During these next 7 Chapters, 7 days, and 7 phrases from the *Disciples' Prayer*, expect to be encountered by God in revelation from His word, in dreams and visions, in increased manifestations of the gifts of the spirit and demonstrations of the Holy Ghost in healings, deliverances and supernatural divine supply and provision. Get ready to experience God the Father, Son and Holy Ghost like you've never experienced Him before, as you enter into the model taught by Jesus for divine encounters to bring heaven to earth.

CHAPTER 6

(DAY 1) OUR FATHER……

– The Fatherhood Anointing

(Sunday-Day 1) - Fast until 6pm and Pray in tongues for 30 minutes and Meditate for 30 minutes Matt 6:1-10; Luke 11:1-13 and on this 1ST phrase from the disciple's prayer; OUR FATHER WHICH IS IN HEAVEN.

TODAY'S MEDITATION: The first realm of access to enter into divine encounters with the glorified Christ is the heavenly realm, accessed through the Father's dimension in prayer. Jesus said, *when you pray, say…****Our father which are in Heaven.*** This phrase in the prayer deals with the aspect of heavenly access into the realm of the spirit by the revelation of God as Father.

The Connection of Jesus' High Priestly Prayer with the Disciples Prayer

This phrase of the *Disciples Prayer* referring to God as Father, "Our Father in Heaven" connects with the High Priestly prayer of Jesus in John 17 at verses 1, 5, 11, 24, 25. *1. These words spake Jesus, and lifted up his eyes to heaven, and said,* ***Father, the hour is come; glorify thy Son****, that thy Son also may glorify thee: 5 And now, **O***

Father, glorify thou me *with thine own self with the glory which I had with thee before the world was. 11.**Holy Father, keep through thine own name** those whom thou hast given me, that they may be one, as we are. Joh 17:24* ***Father, I will that they also, whom thou hast given me, be with me where I am;*** *that they may behold my glory, which thou hast given me: for thou lovedst me before the foundation of the world. 25 O righteous **Father, the world hath not known thee**: but I have known thee, and these have known that thou hast sent me.*

The fatherhood dimension in prayer was a place in prayer that Jesus modeled in His own prayer life. He didn't just teach the disciples to relate to God as father, He related to God as His father. This practice in and of itself is the first step in us becoming one with God and with one another.

Joh 10:30 I and my Father are one.

The very first verse of Matt 6:1 speaks of the necessary practice to enter the fatherhood dimension in prayer to access heaven or the spirit realm. This necessary practice is the practice of focusing on righteousness that God sees and not righteousness that men see.
A father establishes our revelation of righteousness. Your righteousness is a practice that comes from God and is for God. It is a practice done before God for the reward that only God can give, and it is characteristic of having a father.

Matt 6:1 says, beware of practicing your righteousness before men to be noticed by them; otherwise you have no reward with your Father who is in Heaven.

Pro 13:22 A good man leaves an inheritance to his children's children: and the wealth of the sinner is laid up for the righteous.

Righteousness is a practice of the father releasing his name, his character, his inheritance to his children, not based on their good works, or their behavior, but based on their relationship with him as sons and daughters. The righteousness of God is the identity of the believer in Christ before God, in the eyes of God, because of Jesus Christ. The righteousness of God is how God sees every person, both unbelievers and believers alike, in Jesus Christ.

The Characteristics of a Father

Matthew 6:2 So when you give to the poor; do not sound a trumpet before you, as the hypocrites do in the synagogues and in the streets, so that they may be honored by men. Truly I say to you, they have their reward in full. But when you give to the poor, do not let your left hand know what your right hand is doing, so that your giving will be in secret, and your father who sees what is done in secret will reward you.

A Father Teaches You How to Give: Giving is one of the fundamental natures of the character of God, the Father. John 3:16 shows us the nature of God by saying; GOD SO LOVED THE WORLD THAT HE GAVE His ONLY BEGOTTEN SON. Ephesians 5:24 Paul says, Husbands love your wives as Christ Loved the Church and GAVE HIMSELF for it.

One of the 6 things that fathers are to train their children in from Proverbs 22:6 is to GIVE.

Proverbs 22:6 says, train up a child in the way he should go, and even when he is old, he will not depart from it.

Many do not realize in the body of Christ that Jesus training His disciples in prayer is done fundamental and practically by training them in ways that deal with their nature as human beings. These fundamentals of training are found in the verses immediately following Proverbs 22:6, in verses 7-10, and one of those things that children are to be trained in by their fathers is in giving to the poor...*v.8 He who is generous will be blessed, for he gives some of his food to the poor.*

One of the things a father is to train his son or daughter to do is to GIVE. If you have a problem giving it's a father wound. You were never trained in the way of giving. You never received that character from your father. It's the practice of leaving an inheritance for those that you have trained in the ways of God.

This inheritance of giving, that releases the nature of God, also releases the reward of God's righteousness. The practice of righteousness is something you do as result of being before God as father and having released to you the inheritance or reward from father God in Heaven. This is only when giving is done before him, for him, and not to be seen or recognized by men.

But when you give to the poor, do not let your left hand know what your right hand is doing, so that your giving will be in secret, and your father who sees what is done in secret will reward you.

A Father Shares Secrets of Life –

Matthew 6:5 When you pray you are not to be like the hypocrites for they love to stand and pray in the synagogues and on the streets so that they may be seen by men. The second characteristic of a father is fathers teach their disciples about the secrets of God, so that they are acquainted with him, so that they develop faith in him.

Fathers are to show their disciples (children) the Father, God. John 14:8 Phillip said; show us the father; if you do not have a prayer life spending time with God, it could be a by-product of a father wound. Either you didn't have a father, or you didn't spend much time with your father, talking to him, asking him questions and answers, therefore your dialogue with your heavenly father is hindered or in most cases stagnant or non-existent. But as you say, "**OUR FATHER WHICH IS IN HEAVEN**" and begin praying in tongues, meditating on the phrase OUR FATHER, God will heal and reveal your heavenly father's nature as a communicator of truths and mysteries from the secret place. He's a secret teller.

A Father Teaches Forgiveness by Forgiving Us of Our Sins.

Mat 6:14 For if ye forgive men their trespasses, your heavenly Father will also forgive you: Mat 6:15 But if ye forgive not men their trespasses, neither will your Father forgive your trespasses. When a father loves unconditionally, knowing our weaknesses, our short comings, our immaturity, and rebellion, but covers, protects and provides for us, he is releasing the power of forgiveness that causes them to forgive.

A Father Teaches Reliance and Dependence Upon God and His Kingdom

Mat 6:25 Therefore I say unto you, take no thought for your life, what ye shall eat, or what ye shall drink; nor yet for your body, what ye shall put on. Is not the life more than meat, and the body than raiment? 26 Behold the fowls of the air: for they sow not, neither do they reap, nor gather into barns; yet your heavenly Father feeds them. Are ye not much better than they? Mat 6:32 (For after all these things do the Gentiles seek:) for your heavenly Father knows that ye have need of all these things. 33 But seek ye first the kingdom of God, and his righteousness; and all these things shall be added unto you. 34 Take therefore no thought for the morrow: for the morrow shall take thought for the things of itself. Sufficient unto the day is the evil thereof.

The Forgiveness of The Father – Luke 15:11 shows us the heart of the father in forgiveness with the story of the prodigal son. This is the story of two sons, the younger of which asked his father to give him the share of his inheritance, to which the father divided his wealth between them and gave it to them both. After a few days the younger son gathered everything together and went on a journey into a distant country, and there he squandered his estate with loose living. Now when he had spent everything, a severe famine occurred in that country and he began to be impoverished. So, he went and hired himself out to one of the citizens of that country, and he sent him into his fields to feed swine. But when he came to his senses, he said, how many of my father's hired men have more than enough bread, but I am dying here with hunger! I will get up and go to my father, and will say to him, "Father, I have sinned against heaven, and in your sight: I am no longer worthy to be called your son; make me as one of your hired men." So, he got up and came to his father. But while he was still a long way off his father did something the reveals the heart of Father God.

Father God's Heart Revealed. The actions of the father of the prodigal son reveals to us the heart father God to sons and daughters (humanity) that has gone into a far country and has spent all of the inheritance from God the father with riotous living. Luke 15:20...but while he was still a long way off his father saw him and felt compassion for him and ran and embraced him and kissed him. The Father saw him afar off – God the Father sees us no matter how far away we go.

- The father felt compassion from him – God the father has compassion on us in our mess (sin)
- The Father ran to him – God the father runs to us when we make up in our minds to return home
- The Father embraced him – God the father will cover us in our mess from the judgment of outsiders

- The Father kissed him – God the father will kiss us with the kisses of His word to cleanse us from our mess

The Revelation of The Father's Throne (Heaven)

Eph 1:3 Blessed be the God and Father of our Lord Jesus Christ, who hath blessed us with all spiritual blessings in heavenly places in Christ:
Eph 2:6 And hath raised us up together, and made us sit together in heavenly places in Christ Jesus:

Once you get a revelation of the Father which is heaven, He ushers you into heavenly places and causes you to sit in heaven, right where you are in the earth. He transports you there by the spirit into heavenly places.

Heb 12:22 *But ye are come unto mount Sion, and unto the city of the living God, the heavenly Jerusalem, and to an innumerable company of angels,*

Rev 4:1 *After this I looked, and, behold, a door was opened in heaven: and the first voice which I heard was as it were of a trumpet talking with me; which said, come up hither, and I will shew thee things which must be hereafter.*

Rev 4:2 *And immediately I was in the spirit: and, behold, a throne was set in heaven, and one sat on the throne.*

Rev 5:13 *And every creature which is in heaven, and on the earth, and under the earth, and such as are in the sea, and all that are in them, heard I am saying, Blessing, and honor, and glory, and power, be unto him that sits upon the throne, and unto the Lamb for ever and ever.*

When we began praying and saying in the heavenly realm of the Father's dimension in prayer, we will begin seeing the heaven's open and begin hearing the voice of the father saying... *You are my beloved son.* We will also begin seeing visions of the throne of God in heaven, and the worship going on around the throne in heaven. This will enable us to be able to know God's will in heaven, God's revelation of heaven, and God's glory in heaven to be able to bring heaven to earth.

Our Father which Is Heaven...Hallowed by Thy Name.

Heaven is a place of God's presence and God's creatures, and God's people worshipping him for the greatness of His plan for the earth in sending His Son. It is the place where worship goes around the throne, day and night, both from angels and from glorified bodies of those that have lived in the earth in obedience to God's plan and will for their lives. It is the place where the will and plan of God for life is seen to be perfect and true and worshipped as the beautiful plan that only an awesome and Great God could think of.

Rev 4:3 And he that sat was to look upon like a jasper and a sardine stone: and there was a rainbow round about the throne, in sight like unto an emerald.

Rev 4:4 And round about the throne were four and twenty seats: and upon the seats I saw four and twenty elders sitting, clothed in white raiment; and they had on their heads crowns of gold.

Rev 4:5 And out of the throne proceeded lightnings and thundering and voices: and there were seven lamps of fire burning before the throne, which are the seven Spirits of God.

Rev 4:6 And before the throne there was a sea of glass like unto crystal: and in the midst of the throne, and round about the throne, were four beasts full of eyes before and behind.

Rev 4:7 And the first beast was like a lion, and the second beast like a calf, and the third beast had a face as a man, and the fourth beast was like a flying eagle.

Rev 4:8 And the four beasts had each of them six wings about him; and they were full of eyes within: and they rest not day and night, saying, Holy, holy, holy, Lord God Almighty, which was, and is, and is to come.
Rev 4:9 And when those beasts give glory and honor and thanks to him that sat on the throne, who lives for ever and ever,

Rev 4:10 The four and twenty elders fall down before him that sat on the throne, and worship him that lives for ever and ever, and cast their crowns before the throne, saying,

Rev 4:11 Thou art worthy, O Lord, to receive glory and honor and power: for thou hast created all things, and for thy pleasure they are and were created.

INDIVDUAL PRAYER DECLARATION *I declare today that You are my Father. And today I ask that You turn my heart to You as my father. I've learned today that you are a good father. And that You Father by Your Holy Spirit and can heal me of all father wounds I may have from this generation of fatherlessness. Father me God, and heal me of my father wounds, Father me God with your goodness. Father me with your giving nature of love. I've learned that You know how to give good gifts to Your children. I am Your child, and though my earthly fathers may not have had to give to me or knew how to give to me everything I needed, You created me and knew me while I was still in my mother's womb. You know me better than anyone. And You know how to father me from a heavenly perspective. Thank You for being my father in heaven. Let heaven come to me now with Your father's revelation and Love, in Jesus name, Amen.*

(Sunday-day 1) - fast until 6pm and pray in tongues for 30 minutes and meditate for 30 minutes Matt 6:1-10; Luke 11:1-13 and on this 1st phrase from the disciple's prayer; our father which is in heaven.

Scriptural Meditation for Our Father which is in Heaven

Mat 6:1 Take heed that ye do not your alms before men, to be seen of them: otherwise ye have no reward of your Father which is in heaven.

Mat 6:2 Therefore when thou doest thine alms, do not sound a trumpet before thee, as the hypocrites do in the synagogues and in the streets, that they may have glory of men. Verily I say unto you, They have their reward.

Mat 6:3 But when thou doest alms, let not thy left hand know what thy right hand doeth:

Mat 6:4 That thine alms may be in secret: and thy Father which seeth in secret himself shall reward thee openly.
The Lord's Prayer

Mat 6:5 And when thou prayest, thou shalt not be as the hypocrites are: for they love to pray standing in the synagogues and in the corners of the streets, that they may be seen of men. Verily I say unto you, They have their reward.

Mat 6:6 But thou, when thou prayest, enter into thy closet, and when thou hast shut thy door, pray to thy Father which is in secret; and thy Father which seeth in secret shall reward thee openly.

Mat 6:7 But when ye pray, use not vain repetitions, as the heathen do: for they think that they shall be heard for their much speaking.

Mat 6:8 Be not ye therefore like unto them: for your Father knoweth what things ye have need of, before ye ask him.

Mat 6:9 After this manner therefore pray ye: Our Father which art in heaven,
Luke's version of The Lord's Prayer - *Luk 11:1 And it came to pass, that, as he was praying in a certain place, when he ceased, one of his disciples said unto him, Lord, teach us to pray, as John also taught his disciples.*

Luk 11:2 And he said unto them, When ye pray, say, Our Father which art in heaven, Hallowed be thy name. Thy kingdom come. Thy will be done, as in heaven, so in earth.

Luk 11:3 Give us day by day our daily bread.

Luk 11:4 And forgive us our sins; for we also forgive every one that is indebted to us. And lead us not into temptation; but deliver us from evil.

Luk 11:5 And he said unto them, Which of you shall have a friend, and shall go unto him at midnight, and say unto him, Friend, lend me three loaves;

Luk 11:6 For a friend of mine in his journey is come to me, and I have nothing to set before him?

Luk 11:7 And he from within shall answer and say, Trouble me not: the door is now shut, and my children are with me in bed; I cannot rise and give thee.

Luk 11:8 I say unto you, Though he will not rise and give him, because he is his friend, yet because of his importunity he will rise and give him as many as he needeth.

Luk 11:9 And I say unto you, Ask, and it shall be given you; seek, and ye shall find; knock, and it shall be opened unto you.

Luk 11:10 For every one that asketh receiveth; and he that seeketh findeth; and to him that knocketh it shall be opened.

Luk 11:11 If a son shall ask bread of any of you that is a father, will he give him a stone? or if he ask a fish, will he for a fish give him a serpent?

Luk 11:12 Or if he shall ask an egg, will he offer him a scorpion?

Luk 11:13 If ye then, being evil, know how to give good gifts unto your children: how much more shall your heavenly Father give the Holy Spirit to them that ask him?

CORPORATE PRAYER DECLARATION: *We declare today that you are our Father. And today we ask that You turn our hearts to You as our Father. We've learned today that You are a good Father. And that You father us by Your Holy Spirit and heal us of all father wounds we may have from this generation of fatherlessness. Father us God, with your goodness. Father us with your giving nature of love. We've learned that you know how to give good gifts to Your children. We are Your children, and though our earthly fathers may not have had to give to us or knew how to give to us everything we needed, You created us and knew us while we were still in our mother's womb. You know us better than anyone. And You know how to father us with from a heavenly perspective. Thank You for being our Father in heaven. Let heaven come to us now, with the Father's revelation and love, in Jesus name, a*

CHAPTER 7

HALLOWED BE THY NAME

– The Sonship Anointing

(Monday Day 2) - Fast until 6pm and Pray in tongues for 30 minutes and Meditate for 30 minutes on Heb 1:1-4; John 14:6 Matt 1:18-25; Isaiah 9:6 and this 2nd phrase from the disciple's prayer; HALLOWED BE THY NAME)

TODAY'S MEDITATION: The second dimension in entering into encounter prayer is the Son's dimension in prayer, further accessing the heavenly realm. Jesus said, WHEN YOU PRAY, SAY…**Hallowed Be Thy Name**. This level of prayer deals with the aspect of the heavenly access into the realm of the NAME of the father. What is the name of father? This is important because Jesus says to pray…. Our Father, which are in heaven, Hallowed be *THY NAME*.

The Connection of Jesus' High Priestly Prayer with the Disciples Prayer

This phrase of the *Disciples Prayer* "Hallowed be thy Name" connects with the High Priestly prayer of Jesus in John 17 at verse 6, which says, "**I have manifested thy name** unto the men which *you gave me out of the world: thine they were, and you gave them me; and they have kept thy word."* It was the Son's purpose to manifest the Father's name, not His own name. Therefore, as we meditate on *Hallowed be Thy Name*, we are meditating on the purpose and the mission of the Son of God, and the Sonship anointing found in St Luke 4:18. *And when he had opened the book, he found the place where it was written, 18* <u>*The Spirit of the Lord is upon me, because he hath anointed me*</u> *to preach the gospel to the poor; he hath sent me to heal the brokenhearted, to preach deliverance to the captives, and recovering of sight to the blind, to set at liberty them that are bruised, 19 To preach the acceptable year of the Lord.*

This is the anointing that is released when we access the name of God and the power that is resident in that name, as we Hallow or sanctify that name for the purposes it was given for in the earth. It's the name of God that connects God's inheritance as a Father in heaven with His children, the sons of men in the earth. It's the name that connects us with our answers in prayer. It's not because we say the name at the end of our prayers, that we have what we say, but it's because we understand that we are His sons and daughters in the earth and knowing and being in His name assures us that we are truly heirs and joint heirs with Christ. Therefore, knowing the name and being in the name is how we receive our inheritance and answers to our prayers. And according to Jesus' High Priestly prayer, this is how He kept His disciples while He was in the earth, and how He keeps us now.

Holy Father, keep through thine own name those whom thou hast given me, that they may be one, as we are. 12 While I was with them in the world, I kept them in thy name.

This is the anointing from the second phrase of the *Disciples Prayer* that causes us to receive our *Sonship inheritance* and promises, as well as the power that goes with being in the Name. *Php*

2:9 Wherefore God also hath highly exalted him, <u>and given him a name which is above every name: 10 That at the name of Jesus every knee should bow,</u> of things in heaven, and things in earth, and things under the earth; How can we know the name of the father in order to Hallow this name? God has chosen how all would know his name. Hebrews 1:2 says, God, (the father) has spoken unto us by his Son. *1 God, who at sundry times and in divers' manners spoke in time past unto the fathers by the prophets, 2 Hath in these last days spoken unto us by his Son, whom he hath appointed heir of all things, by whom also he made the worlds; Heb 1:3 Who being the brightness of his glory, and the express image of his person, and upholding all things by the word of his power, when he had by himself purged our sins, sat down on the right hand of the Majesty on high; Heb 1:4 Being made so much better than the angels, as he hath by inheritance obtained a more excellent name than they.*

Joh 14:6 Jesus saith unto him, I am the way, the truth, and the life: no man cometh unto the Father, but by me.

To Hallow is the *Greek* word; *hagiazō - hag-ee-ad'-zo, From G40; to make holy, that is, (ceremonially) purify or consecrate; (mentally) to venerate: - hallow, be holy, sanctify.* The Greek word for "Name" is the word "onoma" pronounced; *on'-om-ah; a "name" (literally or figuratively), (authority, character): - called, (+ sur-) name (-d).*

In ancient times, the name of the child was given to envelope the identity and destiny of the child. When you spoke your name in ancient days you were also speaking your destiny, as well as your identity. Several instances in the Bible, names are changed to change destinies and identities of those of whom God would use. – Abram to Abraham, Jacob to Israel, Simon to Peter. Therefore, it should be established that in the name of an individual should reside everything he is, will be, and everything he will accomplish and perform. Therefore, when we talk about the name of the Father, we must understand the name of the Son. The name of the

Son is not just another name different than the father. And it's not just an ordinary name, it's the name of the Christ, which is the body of God in the earth. When we talk about Hallowing the name, it's important to know whose name this prayer is referring to?

"Our father, which is in Heaven, hallowed be THY name……

The name that is being Hallowed is the name of God, the father. This is significant because if He's your father, as the phrase indicates, "Our Father," then whatever is the name of the father, is the name of the son, as well as, the name of whoever is joined to him, either by birth or by adoption. Firstly, as relates to this prayer, we are speaking of the significance of understanding who you are in Him, as your father. Your name signifies your identity, and it determines whether you will receive the inheritance of the father upon His bequeathing of His inheritance. Therefore, understanding the name of God and Hallowing that name as consecrated or holy, or special, is crucial to receiving from God the father in prayer. Therefore, at this level of "saying and praying" it is crucial to receive, knowledge, wisdom and revelation of the name of God, or the name of the father. Because the name of the father is YOUR name as a son or a daughter. And the name determines who you will be, your destiny.

Isaiah 9:6 says, and his name shall be called, Wonderful, Counselor, the Mighty God, the Everlasting Father, the Prince of Peace.

Within the announcement of the name of God was everything God would be and do in heaven and in earth. Isaiah 7:14 says, behold a virgin shall conceive, and bear a son, and shall call his name Immanuel which being interpreted is, God-with us. Understanding the prophetic word given 700 years before Jesus was born gives us insight into what the name of the father is, as well as what the name is we should Hallow from this phrase in the prayer Jesus taught His disciples to pray.

Mat 1:18 Now the birth of Jesus Christ was on this wise: When as his mother Mary was espoused to Joseph, before they came together, she was found with child of the Holy Ghost. 19 Then Joseph her husband, being a just man, and not willing to make her a public example, was minded to put her away privily. **20 But while he thought on these things, behold, the angel of the Lord appeared unto him in a dream, saying, Joseph, thou son of David, fear not to take unto thee Mary thy wife**: *for that which is conceived in her is of the Holy Ghost.* <u>21 And she shall bring forth a son, and thou shalt call his name JESUS: for he shall save his people from their sins.</u> *22 Now all this was done, that it might be fulfilled which was spoken of the Lord by the prophet, saying, 23 Behold, a virgin shall be with child, and shall bring forth a son, and they shall call his name Emmanuel, which being interpreted is, God with us. 24 Then Joseph being raised from sleep did as the angel of the Lord had bidden him and took unto him his wife: 25 And knew her not till she had brought forth her firstborn son: and he called his name JESUS.*

In the Latin, we call His name JESUS, from the Roman Catholic invention and addition of the letter "J." However, the Hebrew name for Jesus is pronounced Yeshua. And Yeshua and Jesus, both mean deliverance or Salvation. However, Yeshua is also the Hebrew word for the Son of God, the Hebrew Messiah. *John 11:25 And she said to Him, "Yes, Lord; I have believed that You are the Christ (Messiah), the Son of the God, even He who comes into the world.* The name "Jesus" appears nowhere in the Greek or Hebrew Scriptures. The letter "J" was invented in the 1500's, and shortly thereafter, the Roman Catholic Church revised the Name of the Messiah, changing it to Jesus.

In our ministry we a have specific calling to pray for Israel, and for the eyes of God's firstborn son, Israel to come to the revelation of Messiah. We pray for the revelation of Messiah to come to the Jews, because Yeshua bound himself to only return whenever the

Jewish leadership would say, "Blessed is He that comes in the name of Lord." Matt. 23:39 *For I say to you, from now on you will not see Me until you say, "Blessed is He who comes in the name of the Lord."*

Was the Name of the Son Given from Heaven or The Earth?

There are many people that think that the name Yeshua or Jesus has no significance in and of itself. Many people believe that the name Yeshua is only of significance with the added "Christ" following it as such, "Jesus Christ." There are many that believe that the name Yeshua alone has no power or relevance apart from the Christ, which means the Christas, or the Anointed one. They say that the child, Yeshua was born, but the Son, "Christ" was given. However, Matthew 1:18 says. Now the birth of Jesus Christ (Yeshua) was on this wise: not the birth of Jesus (Yeshua) was on this wise, but Jesus Christ, Yeshua. Many believe that Yeshua was simply his earthly name and that there's no power or significance in Yeshua's name apart from "Christ." The Deliverance of the Name Yeshua. The name of Yeshua didn't come from Mary; the name of Yeshua didn't come from Joseph. The Bible says in Matthew that the angel delivered to Joseph what the name of the promised child would be. inis angei was Gabriel, one of the arch angels of God known as the messenger angel. This messenger angel was assigned to take messages from God to man throughout the Old Testament. A very familiar depiction of the messenger angel Gabriel was when Daniel prayed and fasted 21 days. After the 21st day the messenger angel Gabriel arrived with Daniel's prayer answer from God. When John the Baptist was born, the messenger angel Gabriel arrived with the message from God that Zacharias and Elisabeth would have a child and his name shall be called John (which means God has been gracious). The name Yeshua didn't come from man, it came from God. Yeshua said in John 17:6, 7 have manifested or revealed thy name unto the men -which you gave me out of the world'. Hebrews 1:1-4 says, God who at sundry times and in divers manners spoke in time past unto the fathers by the prophets, hath in these last days spoken unto us by his Son, whom he hath appointed heir of all things, by whom also he made the worlds; who being the brightness of his glory, and the express image of his person, and upholding all things by the word of his power, when he had by himself purged our sins, sat down on the right hand of the majesty on high; being made so much better than the angels, AS HE HATH BY INHERITANCE OBTAINED A MORE EXCELLENT NAME THAN THEY.

The name of Yeshua was inherited from the Father. The name of Yeshua was not given from the earth but from heaven. The name Yeshua in the Greek is the name "Jehoshua" - the name of our Lord. Jehoshua is a derivative of the name Joshua as recorded in Numbers 13:16 saying, And Moses catted O-she-a (Joshua) the son of Nun, Jehoshua. Jehoshua is a Hebrew word "Yehowsheba" which means Jehovah - the self-existent or Eternal, which is the Jewish national name of God. It also means Jehovah - saved which means to defend, deliver, help, preserve, rescue, be safe, bring (having) salvation, savior, get victory. These meanings come from the combination of the Hebrew words "Ye hovah-yasha" or "Ye howshua" which is JEHOVAH GOD of the Old Testament.

Therefore, when we talk about who Yeshua is we must understand the name of Yeshua. The name Yeshua is not just another name. It is not just an ordinary name. However, just because you have the name doesn't necessarily make you what the name possesses and suggests. It's in who has given you the name and where the name has come from as well as your relationship to the giver of the name that brings the significance, authority, power and right to the named.

Jehovah of the Old Testament Is the Yeshua of the New Testament

All the compound names of Jehovah in the Old Testament are all wrapped up and fulfilled in Yeshua. That's why Isaiah says about this child that would be born and this son that would be given; His name shall be called Mighty God, Everlasting Father. In the name Yeshua is everything that was expressed through all the compound names of Jehovah in the Old Testament, our Father.

In the name Yeshua was every attribute and character ascribed to God the Father in the Old Testament. God began to progressively reveal His person and nature to Abraham as Jehovah-Jireh, the Lord will provide. To Moses, I AM that I AM, which is the Hebrew word *"hayah"* which means to exist, or be, or become, come to pass, altogether be. As God began to progressively reveal Himself to the patriarchs it was as if He was keeping back from them in each generation His fullness, or His glory, realizing that they would not be able to stand it. This is seen in God's words to Moses when he asked God, in Exodus 33:18, Shew me thy glory. The Hebrew word for glory is "kabod," which means weight or fullness, honor, richness.

Moses wanted to see Yeshua. Moses wanted a complete revelation of Jehovah. Moses wanted to see God's fullness. Exodus 33:19 God said, I will make all my goodness pass before thee, and I will proclaim the name of the Lord before thee: and will be gracious to whom I will be gracious and will shew mercy on whom I will shew mercy. Actually, God was saying here that what you're asking for Moses is reserved for the people of the Church age. A mature people that will be prepared to inherit the fullness of God in receiving His name as completing the progressive revelation of Jehovah in the Old Testament, of whom I will have mercy upon and reveal My fullness to. *Then He said, thou canst not see My face: for there shall no man see Me and live. And the Lord said, Behold, there is a place by Me, and thou shall stand on a rock.*

Mat 16:16 And Simon Peter answered and said, Thou art the Christ, the Son of the living God. 17 And Jesus answered and said unto him, Blessed art thou, Simon Barjona: for flesh and blood hath not revealed it unto thee, but my Father which is in heaven.

Mat 16:18 And I say also unto thee, that thou art Peter, and upon this rock I will build my church; and the gates of hell shall not prevail against it.

God would not reveal the totality of His name to that generation, but He would unravel and unroll it like a scroll to mankind, revealing a piece to every generation, culminating in the Yeshua generation with the revelation of His complete nature in the name of Yeshua, and the life of Yeshua. In the name of Yeshua are all of the compound names of Jehovah in the Old Testament. In the name of Yeshua is the fullness of the Godhead. In the life of Yeshua he perfectly fulfilled the character and function of each compound name of Jehovah.

Below is listed the Old Testament compound names of Jehovah, along with its meaning, function or character. Alongside is the fulfillment in the New Testament of each compound name in the life of Yeshua with the scripture in which each character was fulfilled.

The Jehovah of the Old, the Yeshua of the New
- Jehovah - Jireh - the Lord our Provider (Gen. 22:14)---------Yeshua our Provider --(Heb. 10:12)
- Jehovah - Tsidkenu - the Lord our Righteousness (Jer. 23:6, 33:16)--Yeshua our Righteousness --(I Corinth. 1:30)
- Jehovah - Shammah - Lord is Present (Ezk. 48:25)-------------Yeshua is always Present---(Matt 28:20)

- Jehovah - Rapha - the Lord our Healer (Exo. 15:26)------Yeshua is our Healer-------(James 5:14)
- Jehovah - Mkeddish - the Lord our Sanctifier (Ex 31:13)---------Yeshua is our Sanctifier---(Eph 5:23-26)
- Jehovah - Raah -the Lord our Shepherd (Ps. 23:1)-----------------Yeshua is our Shepherd-----(John 10:1)
- Jehovah - Nissi - the Lord our Banner, Victory (Ex 17:15)--------Yeshua is our Victory --------(I Cor. 1   5:57)
- Jehovah - Sabboth - the Lord of Host (Joshua 5:13)--------------Yeshua is the Captain of the Host—James (5:4)
- Jehovah - Shalom -the Lord our Peace (Jud. 6:24)--------------- --Yeshua is our Peace----(John 14:27)
- Jehovah - Hoseenu - the Lord our Maker (Gen. 1:1)-------------Yeshua is our Maker-------(Colossian 1:16)
- Jehovah - Elyon - the Lord Most High (Ps. 47:2)-----------------Yeshua is the Most High (Luke 1:32,76)

This is how Yeshua could truly and correctly say in John 14:9, He that hath seen me hath seen the Father. This is why Yeshua could say I and my Father are one. Because the attributes, the nature and character of the Father was manifested in the life of Yeshua because of whose name He had and His relationship with He of whom He received the name from.

Again, the name determines who you will be, your destiny. Isaiah 9:6 *says, and his name (Yeshua) shall be called, Wonderful, Counselor, the Mighty God, the Everlasting Father, the Prince of Peace*. Within the name Yeshua was everything God would be and do in heaven and in earth. Isaiah 7:14 says, *behold a virgin shall conceive, and bear a son, and shall call his name (Yeshua) Immanuel, which being interpreted is, God - with us.*

The actual Hebrew rendering of the name Immanuel is, "with us God, or equally God with us." God was able to be equally with us while yet being in heaven at the same time because of His name. His name denotes His abilities, His attributes and His character. This is why Deuteronomy 6:4 can say;

Hear O Israel: The Lord our God is one Lord and yet 1 John 5:7 says, for there are three that bear record in heaven, the Father, the Word, and the Holy Ghost; and these are one.

The name of Yeshua is what enables these three to be one. The identity of every title or office God would assume and fulfill was wrapped up in His name. This is why he instructed the Disciples to baptize in the name of the Father, and of the Son, and of the Holy Ghost; and yet on the day of Pentecost the disciples instructed all Believers to be baptized in Yeshua's Name. They understood that Yeshua was not only the name of the Son, but that the Son inherited that name from the Father. Therefore, they realized that the name of Yeshua was like the Budweiser commercials some years ago; WHEN YOU'VE SAID YESHUA YOU'VE SAID IT ALL (Father, Son and Holy Ghost).

TODAY'S INDIVDUAL PRAYER DECLARATION *I declare today that your name is hallowed. I declare today that Your name is Holy. I declare today that Your name is great. And today I ask that you to manifest Your great name in my life. I've learned today that everything I need is found in Your name. My healing, victory, provision, is all found in Your name. And I thank You that You sent Your Son to reveal Your name to me. In the name of Jesus and by the power of Your Holy Spirit reveal and release Your name to me. Reveal and release my sonship nature to me. I am Your Son, and I am an heir with Christ and through the name of Jesus, I have entered into the blessing of Abraham. I receive my sonship inheritance in Jesus name, I receive my healing in Jesus name. I receive victory over all of my enemies in Jesus name. I receive provision for my life in Jesus name. I receive everything You sent Your Son to die to give me today in Jesus name. Amen. (now pray in tongues)*

(Monday Day 2) - Fast until 6pm and Pray in tongues for 30 minutes and Meditate for 30 minutes on Heb 1:1-4; John 14:6

Matt 1:18-25; Isaiah 9:6 and this 2nd phrase from the disciple's prayer; HALLOWED BE THY NAME)

Scriptural Meditation for Hallowed Be Thy Name

Heb 1:1 *God, who at sundry times and in divers manners spake in time past unto the fathers by the prophets,*

Heb 1:2 <u>Hath in these last days spoken unto us by his Son, whom he hath appointed heir of all things, by whom also he made the worlds;</u>

Heb 1:3 *Who being the brightness of his glory, and the express image of his person, and upholding all things by the word of his power, when he had by himself purged our sins, sat down on the right hand of the Majesty on high;*

Heb 1:4 *Being made so much better than the angels, as he hath by* **<u>inheritance obtained a more excellent name than they.</u>**

Joh 14:6 *Jesus saith unto him, I am the way, the truth, and the life: no man cometh unto the Father, but by me.*

Joh 14:7 *If ye had known me, ye should have known my Father also: and from henceforth ye know him, and have seen him.*

Joh 14:8 *Philip saith unto him, Lord, shew us the Father, and it suffice us.*

Joh 14:9 *Jesus saith unto him, Have I been so long time with you, and yet hast thou not known me, Philip? he that hath seen me hath seen the Father; and how says thou then, Shew us the Father?*

TODAY'S CORPORATE *PRAYER DECLARATION* We declare today that your name is hallowed. We declare today that Your name is

Holy. We declare today that Your name is great. And today We ask that you to manifest Your great name in my life. We've learned today that everything We need is found in Your name. Our healing, victory, provision, is all found in Your name. And we thank You that You sent Your Son to reveal Your name to us. In the name of Jesus and by the power of Your Holy Spirit reveal and release Your name to us. Reveal and release our sonship nature to us. We are Your Sons, and We are heirs with Christ and through the name of Jesus, we have entered into the blessing of Abraham. We receive our sonship inheritance in Jesus name, we receive our healing in Jesus name. We receive victory over all of our enemies in Jesus name. We receive provision for our lives in Jesus name. We receive everything Your Son to die to give me today in Jesus name. Amen. (now pray in tongues)

When You Pray Say

CHAPTER 8

(DAY 3) - THY KINGDOM COME THY WILL BE DONE –

The Holy Ghost Anointing in Prayer

{Tuesday Day 3) - Fast until 6pm and Pray in tongues for 30 minutes and Meditate for 30 minutes on Romans 14:17; I Cor 14:14; Ephesians 2:14; Hebrews 12:2; Matthews 6:33, and this 3RD phrase from the disciple's prayer; THY KINGDOM COME THY WILL BE DONE IN EARTH AS IT IS IN HEAVEN)

TODAY'S MEDITATION: The third dimension to entering into encounter prayer is the Holy Ghost's dimension in prayer, accessing the Kingdom realm, to bring heaven to earth. Jesus said, "When you pray, say" ...*Thy kingdom Come, thy will be done...* This level of prayer deals with the aspect of kingdom access into the realm of the Holy Spirit's dimension in prayer, to bring what has been seen in heaven, to the earth.

The Connection of Jesus' High Priestly Prayer with the Disciples Prayer

This phrase of the *Disciples Prayer* "Thy Kingdom Come, thy will be done in earth as it is in heaven." connects with the High Priestly prayer of Jesus in John 17 at verse 4, saying, *I have glorified thee on the earth: I have finished the work which you gave me to do.* This is the Holy Ghost anointing that empowers every believer to be a witness of the kingdom of God to be able to release the kingdom of God that's within by way of spiritual vision, from heaven to the earth to glorify the Father and the Son, bringing the heavenly realm into the earth realm.

What is the kingdom of God and where is it located? Romans 14:17 tells us what the kingdom of God is, when Paul tells the Roman Church that the kingdom of God is righteousness, peace and Joy <u>in the Holy Ghost</u>. **The kingdom of God is in the Holy Ghost, and as we pray meditative prayers concerning the kingdom of God**, both with the spirit and with the understanding, we release God's kingdom from heaven to us and through us into earth.

Rom 14:17 For the kingdom of God is not meat and drink; but righteousness, and peace, and joy in the Holy Ghost.

1Co 14:14 For if I pray in an unknown tongue, my spirit prays, but my understanding is unfruitful. 15 What is it then? I will pray with the spirit, and I will pray with the understanding also:

The process of getting the kingdom of God within us, is the process of understanding the will of the father, and the word and name of the Son, from the first two phrases; "Our Father in Heaven, and "Hallowed be thy Name," to cause us to pray that will and word into the earth realm from the heavenly realm.

This process is a two-fold ministry, called in scripture, the ministry of reconciliation (2 Cor. 5:18,19; Eph. 2:11) of calling heaven back to earth, and the ministry of peace, which is what Romans 14:17 is referring to when it says, the Kingdom of God is righteousness, peace and joy in the Holy Ghost. Peace in that verse is the Greek word eirēnē, which means to set at one again. The word,

"Reconciliation" in 2 Cor. 5:18 is the Greek word "katallassō" which means atonement, or to compound a difference. So the process of getting understanding and praying "Thy Kingdom come, thy will be done" is the process of conjoining heaven and earth in the Son, who is our peace, for His reign to begin, never to end.

2Co 5:18 And all things are of God, who hath reconciled us to himself by Jesus Christ, and hath given to us the ministry of reconciliation; 19 To wit, that God was in Christ, reconciling the world unto himself, not imputing their trespasses unto them; and hath committed unto us the word of reconciliation. 20 Now then we are ambassadors for Christ, as though God did beseech you by us: we pray you in Christ's stead, be ye reconciled to God.

Eph 2:14 For he is our peace, who hath made both one, and hath broken down the middle wall of partition between us; 15 Having abolished in his flesh the enmity, even the law of commandments contained in ordinances; for to make in himself of twain one new man, so making peace; 16 And that he might reconcile both unto God in one body by the cross, having slain the enmity thereby...

With the kingdom of God being defined in Romans 14:17, as righteousness, peace and joy, we can see that the power of a substantive prayer life is wrapped up in having a righteousness consciousness, a peace consciousness and a joy consciousness, as well as being filled with the Holy Ghost.

We Discern the Will of God by Pursuing the Heart of God

19 years ago, my heart was broken as God directed me to close down my father's Church in the inner-city of Columbus Ohio. I had been recently installed as the Pastor and was contemplating how to proceed when God said, *"This is not My will for your life."* My heart was broken thinking about how to let go of what many people, both family and friends, thought was God's will for my life.

To begin healing my heart God began revealing to me what it takes to know the will of God for my life – you must be a man after His heart from Acts 13:22. *I found David, a man after mine own heart which shall fulfill all of my will.*

This sent me on a personal research and quest to try to locate the heart of God, and His peace in my life when I realized that I had no peace doing my own thing. This sent me on a study and a quest after God's heart, after mine was revealed to be after the works of the fleshly ambition in ministry. It began as a quest to get rid of every vestige of selfishness and carnality in my life. It started out as a quest to know God's Heart in order to accomplish all of his will for my life.

It all began in 1999 after God instructed me to close down my father's church in the inner-city of Columbus Ohio. While dealing with the brokenness of my heart and life, I was reading in the book of Acts and came across Acts 13:22; *I found David, a man after mine own heart which shall fulfill all of my will.* After I read that verse, I was totally engulfed with the question in my spirit, "*How does a man receive a testimony from God that he fulfilled all of God's will in his generation*?

As I read that verse, I realized the process of God looking for a man that would fulfill all of His will. The verse begins with, *After He removed Saul, He raised up David to be their King*, concerning whom He said, I have found David, the son of Jesse, A MAN AFTER MY OWN HEART, WHO WILL DO ALL OF MY WILL.

The process of knowing and doing the will of God, over your own will or fleshly ambition, is the process of firstly, removing Saul off the throne of your heart and life. The Saul Syndrome is the syndrome of people pleasing, appearance ministry, and doing ministry for what you will receive now in this life, before men, as opposed to doing for heavenly rewards. Saul disobeyed the prophet Samuel three times, because of his preoccupation with what the people thought, or how it would make Him look before the people. Removing Saul from the throne is the first step in receiving the Davidic commendation, *I have found David, A man after My own heart, who will fulfill all of My will.*

The second step from these verses to knowing and fulfilling the will of God for my life is being Found of God. How did God find David? Where was David when God found Him? David was in the sheepfold tending His father's flock, worshipping. God will always find worshippers. He will always find those that are serving fathers. If we're going to be a man after God's heart, we're going to have to serve fathers, turning our hearts back to fathers in the faith and looking to serve their visions. It's as we are serving Fathers in the faith that we receive the heart of Father God. I believe God is releasing the spirit of Elijah back into the earth in this season, turning the hearts of the fathers to their children, and the hearts of the children to the fathers to release the coming of the kingdom of God into the earth.

Mal 4:5 Behold, I will send you Elijah the prophet before the coming of the great and dreadful day of the LORD: 6 And he shall turn the heart of the fathers to the children, and the heart of the children to their fathers, lest I come and smite the earth with a curse.

Worship is serving and serving is worship, and as David served His father's flock, God gave David the Father's heart. To receive a heart after God, we must serve Fathers, as worship unto God, to receive God's heart to fulfill all of God's will.

Once I read that verse, I was forever ruined from remaining the same, continuing in the state of pursuing my own desires, being satisfied with doing my own thing. A voice spoke up in my spirit, *"You must pursue the Heart of God, not your own ministry, or ministry success."* I then replied, "What is the Heart of God?

These two questions began to consume my thoughts and heart. What I found out over the next 18 months of my life was astounding to my understanding. It totally revolutionized my concept of success in ministry, and what the will of God for my life was. The things that were shown to me by God made me, more than ever before, desirous of one thing, to pray to receive the Heart of God, to pray for his kingdom to come and his will to be done in me, as it was in him. If I never preached another sermon or sung another song, if I could just get that heart, He had revealed to me was His heart, to see in the earth what was revealed in my spirit through the prayer of brokenness. I no longer cared who spoke it, who built it, or who preached it. It no longer had to be me. All I wanted to do was pray day and night, *"Thy Kingdom come, thy will be done, in me as it is in you, in earth as it is in heaven."*

The Kingdom of God Will Come Through the Heart of God

The heart of God and the preceding kingdom of God, as revealed to me over the next 18 months, became the longing of my heart - *A covenant community with the foundation of God's righteousness, peace and Joy in the Holy Ghost as its cornerstone.* A Covenant community that would bring forth a people that truly related with God and one another in right standing and at peace with one another, Black, White, rich, poor, protestant, catholic, Jew, Gentile, Arab, Israeli, all coming together in one body, the body of Christ. A people that truly loved the Lord thy God with all their heart, mind, soul and strength, and loved their neighbor as themselves. This became my longing desire and my deepest prayer.

Therefore, the meditative process of saying, and praying the phrase "Thy kingdom come, thy will be done"...is the process of meditating on being in right standing with our fellowman, through the Righteousness of God which is ours in Christ, the Peace of God that surpasses all understanding, and the Joy of the Lord, which is our strength (Nehemiah 8:11). This will enable us to overcome our sin consciousness synonymous with our sin nature, enabling us to guard our hearts and minds from anxiety, fear and worry, with the peace of God, and enabling us to endure with the *Joy of the Lord*, the trials and tribulations synonymous with taking up our cross and following Christ.

TRANSFORMATIVE

2Co 5:21 For he hath made him to be sin for us, who knew no sin; that we might be made the righteousness of God in him.

Php. 4:6 Be careful (anxious) about nothing; but in everything by prayer and supplication with thanksgiving let your requests be made known unto God. 7 And the peace of God, which passes all understanding, shall keep your hearts and minds through Christ Jesus.

Heb. 12:2 Looking unto Jesus the author and finisher of our faith; who for the joy that was set before him endured the cross, despising the shame, and is set down at the right hand of the throne of God.

Neh. 8:10 for this day is holy unto our Lord: neither be ye sorry; for the joy of the LORD is your strength.

The Righteousness Consciousness of The Kingdom of God

Mat 6:33 <u>But seek ye first the kingdom of God, and his righteousness</u>; and all these things shall be added unto you.

Rom 1:16 For I am not ashamed of the gospel of Christ: for it is the power of God unto salvation to everyone that believeth; to the Jew first, and also to the Greek. 17 <u>For therein is the righteousness of God revealed from faith to faith: as it is written, the just shall live by faith.</u> 18 For the wrath of God is revealed from heaven against all ungodliness and unrighteousness of men, who hold the truth in unrighteousness;

The word righteousness comes from the original Greek word, "dikaiosune" which means; equity (of character or act); specifically (Christian) justification. Justification means to be placed in right standing through the moral, equity and character of Christ.

The good news is not only that Jesus died for our sins, but that His death, burial and resurrection brought us into right standing (righteousness) with God and gave us access to God to receive new life or a fresh start, before our behavior lines up with this reality. However, for the believer and follower of Christ God has given to us the righteousness of Christ. Here are the two things you need to know about God and righteousness.

First - God has Imputed to us the Righteousness of Christ. Impute means to credit it to someone's account. God has given to us the righteousness of Christ. He has taken the list of all of our sins, past, present, and future and declared all our sins forgiven and all our debts paid. It's like if I showed up at your front door and handed you the deed to the house and the statement from the mortgage company and stamped on it *Paid in Full*.

When we accept Christ to be our Savior, God the Father gives to us the righteousness of Christ. He takes our sins and places them on Jesus on the cross and takes Jesus's righteousness and gives it to you.

Second - God Imparts to us the Righteousness of Christ. This is the work of the Holy Spirit helping you to live a righteous life. The Spirit is in us to help us choose to make righteous decisions by the power of the Spirit instead of us walking in the flesh and continuing to sin. ***Pro 13:22 A good man leaves an inheritance to his children's children: and the wealth of the sinner is laid up for the righteous.*** **Righteousness is a covenant word** which means to be in right standing. It means to be declared just or innocent. It means to be identified with the one you are connected to.

It also is a word that determines your positioning for the inheritance. It's a word that identifies you with the prosperity of who you relate to. If you are righteous it means you are in line for the inheritance.

The Peace Consciousness of The Kingdom of God

Eph. 2:14 For he is our peace, who hath made both one, and hath broken down the middle wall of partition between us; 15 Having abolished in his flesh the enmity, even the law of commandments contained in ordinances; for to make in himself of twain one new man, so making peace;

Jesus is our peace or reconciliation in the Kingdom of God. And this peace is in the Holy Ghost, because the Kingdom is in the Holy Ghost (Ro.14:17). Therefore, if you don't pray in the Holy Ghost you will struggle, not only with your flesh, but with your fleshly, ethnic expression of the gospel. Your Christian expression will be dominated by your racial experience or expression and not a true kingdom expression of our faith in Christ. The Holy Ghost is the power to express Christs' expression of the kingdom over your White, Black, Conservative, Liberal, Capitalist, Communist, or Socialist expression of the Kingdom. We must live, preach and manifest the Kingdom expression of our faith in Christ over our racial or political expression, through the power of the Holy Ghost....praying in the Holy Ghost. This is what was revealed to Peter in Acts 10, through the Holy Ghost.

Opening his mouth, Peter said: "I most certainly understand now that God is not one to show partiality, but in every nation the man who fears Him and does what is right is welcome to Him. The word which He sent to the sons of Israel, PREACHING PEACE through Jesus Christ (He is Lord of all)- Acts 10:34-36 NASB

In the context of Peter being delivered from bigotry and racism

Peter received the revelation of the message he was sent by God to preach to ALL, both Jews and Gentiles...Preaching PEACE (Reconciliation of all nations) through Jesus Christ.

The Joy Consciousness of The Kingdom of God

Heb. 12:2 Looking unto Jesus the author and finisher of our faith; who <u>for the joy that was set before him endured the cross</u>, despising the shame, and is set down at the right hand of the throne of God.

Neh. 8:10 for this day is holy unto our Lord: neither be ye sorry; for <u>the joy of the LORD is your strength.</u>

The Joy consciousness of the kingdom of God is that which we receive from the spirit to endure the persecution and tribulation that we must endure to enter into the kingdom of God...*and that we must through much tribulation enter into the kingdom of God (Acts 14:22).* Every believer has a cross to bear. Every believer must go through tribulation in life, and the Joy of the Lord is our strength to go through whatever we must go through to enter into the place and position God has for us in His kingdom. As Jesus endured His cross *for the Joy that was set before Him*, we also will endure our cross through that same joy set before us. This aspect of the kingdom combats the enemies from without, that are set against us. While the righteousness consciousness of the kingdom combats our sin nature, and the peace consciousness combats tendency to fear, have anxiety and worry in our minds as we are transitioning from the kingdom of darkness to the kingdom of God, the joy consciousness combats people that come against us, eventually attempting to crucify, and literally kill us as was the case with Jesus on Calvary. However, through the Joy of the Lord, we're able to endure our cross.

Joh 16:21 A woman when she is in travail hath sorrow, because her hour is come: <u>but as soon as she is delivered of the child, she</u>

remembers no more the anguish, for joy that a man is born into the world.

Joh 16:33 These things I have spoken unto you, that in me ye might have peace. In the world ye shall have tribulation: but be of good cheer; I have overcome the world.

Our propensity to avoid trouble, tribulation and persecution comes from the absence of the revelation of the gospel of kingdom joy. We have not preached the joy of Kingdom of God that's manifested to combat persecution, tribulation and attack associated with bearing our cross in a hostile world. When we truly return the gospel of the kingdom and begin preaching joy that combats tribulation, righteousness that combats our sin nature and Peace that combats fear, we will be fit for the long haul to endure to the end regardless of whether we are raptured out at the beginning, middle or the end of the tribulation.

The Kingdom of God Is Within You (In the Holy Ghost)

Mat. 12:28 But if I cast out devils by the Spirit of God, then the kingdom of God is come unto you.

Mat. 25:34 Then shall the King say unto them on his right hand, Come, ye blessed of my Father, inherit the kingdom prepared for you from the foundation of the world:

Luk. 17:21 Neither shall they say, lo here! or, lo there! for, behold, the kingdom of God is within you.

The purpose of the power of the Holy Ghost causes you to walk in the truth of the teachings of Kingdom of God, as a witness of what's coming to the earth when the King returns to rule and reign in righteousness. We need power to walk out the Kingdom truths in our lives, in the midst of a counterculture society that is antithetical (opposite life philosophy) to the Kingdom of God.

In Acts 1:6 His disciples asked Him, *"Is this the time you will restore the Kingdom?"* Jesus said, *"It's not for you the know the seasons and times the father has put in his own power*...But YOU SHALL RECEIVE POWER AFTER THE HOLY GHOST HAS COME UPON YOU AND YOU SHALL BE WITNESSES UNTO ME (to live the truths of the Kingdom of God) FIRST IN JERUSALEM...AND TO THE UTMOST PARTS OF THE EARTH.

The power of the Holy Ghost is for the purpose of living in the Kingdom, before the Kingdom comes, as a light to the kingdom of darkness, as to what's imminently coming to replace the present system operating in the earth. If we only relegate the power of the Holy Ghost to the gifts and the anointing to do works in the kingdom, and not the power to live in Kingdom righteousness, peace and joy in the Holy Ghost, we short circuit the power of God in us, and we fall short of God's purpose for sending the Holy Ghost – *To be a witness of Christ and His kingdom and the earth before it fully comes.*

TODAY'S INDIVDUAL PRAYER DECLARATION *I declare today that Your kingdom comes, and Your will is done in my life today as it is in You. I declare today that Your kingdom is righteousness peace and joy in the Holy Ghost. I declare that Your kingdom is within me, and that I walk in a righteousness consciousness and not a sin consciousness. I walk in a peace consciousness and not a worry, fear or anxiety consciousness. I walk in a joy consciousness and not a persecution or martyr consciousness. Today I am a witness of Your kingdom in the earth, until it comes in fulness. I seek first the kingdom of God and all of Your righteousness, and all things need for life and godliness are added to me. Today I am in the kingdom by the power of the Holy Ghost, and my gifts, my fruit and my faith are all given to me to live out kingdom realities in the midst of a* *counterculture kingdom in this world. Make me a person after Your own heart that I may do all of your will for my generation, in Jesus name.*

{Tuesday Day 3) - Fast until 6pm and Pray in tongues for 30 minutes and Meditate for 30 minutes on Romans 14:17; I Cor 14:14; Ephesians 2:14; Hebrews 12:2; Matthews 6:33, and this 3RD phrase from the disciple's prayer; THY KINGDOM COME THY WILL BE DONE IN EARTH AS IT IS IN HEAVEN)

Scriptural Meditation for Thy Kingdom Come...

Rom 14:17 For the kingdom of God is not meat and drink; but righteousness, and peace, and joy in the Holy Ghost.

Mat 6:33 <u>But seek ye first the kingdom of God, and his righteousness</u>; and all these things shall be added unto you.
16 For I am not ashamed of the gospel of Christ: for it is the power of God unto salvation to everyone that believeth; to the Jew first, and also to the Greek. 17 <u>For therein is the righteousness of God revealed from faith to faith: as it is written, the just shall live by faith.</u> 18 For the wrath of God is revealed from heaven against all ungodliness and unrighteousness of men, who hold the truth in unrighteousness;

1Co 14:14 For if I pray in an unknown tongue, my spirit prays, but my understanding is unfruitful. 15 What is it then? I will pray with the spirit, and I will pray with the understanding also:

2Co 5:18 And all things are of God, who hath reconciled us to himself by Jesus Christ, and hath given to us the ministry of reconciliation; 19 To wit, that God was in Christ, reconciling the world unto himself, not imputing their trespasses unto them; and hath committed unto us the word of reconciliation. 20 Now then we are ambassadors for Christ, as though God did beseech you by us: we pray you in Christ's stead, be ye reconciled to God.

Eph 2:14 For he is our peace, who hath made both one, and hath broken down the middle wall of partition between us; 15 Having abolished in his flesh the enmity, even the law of commandments contained in ordinances; for to make in himself of twain one new man, so making peace; 16 And that he might reconcile both unto God in one body by the cross, having slain the enmity thereby...

Heb. 12:2 Looking unto Jesus the author and finisher of our faith; who for the joy that was set before him endured the cross, despising the shame, and is set down at the right hand of the throne of God.

TODAY'S CORPORATE *PRAYER DECLARATION* We declare today that Your kingdom comes, and Your will is done in our lives today as it is in You. We declare today that Your kingdom is righteousness peace and joy in the Holy Ghost. We declare that Your kingdom is within us, and that we walk in a righteousness consciousness and not a sin consciousness. We walk in a peace consciousness and not a worry, fear or anxiety consciousness. We walk in a joy consciousness and not a persecution or martyr consciousness. Today, we are witnesses of Your kingdom in the earth, until it comes in fulness. We seek first the kingdom of God and all of Your righteousness, and all things needed for life and godliness are added to us. Today we are in the kingdom by the power of the Holy Ghost, and my gifts, my fruit and my faith are all given to me to live out kingdom realities in the midst of a counterculture kingdom in this world. Make us people after Your own heart that we may do all of your will for our generation, in Jesus name.

CHAPTER 9

(DAY 4) GIVE US THIS DAY OUR DAILY BREAD –

The Anointing of the Word and Supernatural living

(Wednesday Day 4) - Fast until 6pm and Pray in tongues for 30 minutes and Meditate for 30 minutes on Deut. 8:1-5; Matt 4:4; Gen. 42:25; and this 4TH phrase from the disciple's prayer; GIVE US THIS DAY OUR DAILY BREAD)

TODAY'S MEDITATION: The fourth dimension in prayer is the earthly realm of the Word's dimension in prayer. "When you pray, say" ...**Give us this day our daily bread**... This level of prayer deals with the aspect of the supernatural provision of God that God releases to His people as He's transitioning them from one realm to another, *from Egypt to their promised land, from sin to righteousness, from the kingdom of darkness to the kingdom of God and His Son.*

The Connection of Jesus' High Priestly Prayer with the Disciples Prayer

This phrase of the *Disciples Prayer* "Give us this day our daily Bread" connects with the High Priestly prayer of Jesus in John 17 at verse 8, which says, *"For I have given unto them the words which you gave me; and they have received them, and have known surely that I came out from thee, and they have believed that thou didst send me."* Bread in scripture is symbolic of the word of God, and it is what we feed our spirit-man on to grow and go from our wilderness to our promised land. When Jesus directed us to pray for daily bread, He was directing us to ask for an appetite for the word of God as bread from heaven for our spirit, as He rained down bread from heaven daily for the children of Israel during their wilderness wanderings.

Then said the Lord unto Moses, Behold, I will rain bread from heaven for you; and the people shall go out and gather a certain rate every day, that I may prove them, whether they will walk in my law, or not. We have come to a very a critical time in the church in our nation. Exodus 16:7

Just like the children of Israel were to live off God's provision sent from heaven early every morning and in the evening, and not look to take any more than they could eat for that day, we are to seek God early for our daily bread as the manna that was supernaturally released from heaven for them in the wilderness. The manna from heaven in the wilderness is comparable to the word from God to our soul.

Mat 4:4 But he answered and said, It is written, Man shall not live by bread alone, but by every word that proceeds out of the mouth of God.

If they were disciplined to live off just enough of what God sent daily from heaven, they would one day live in the land of more than enough in the promised land. This was God's Holy Ghost budget that they were to live by. *It is not until you learn to be faithful over the little day by day that God gives, will you make it to the land of plenty.* God told the children of Israel in the wilderness to take only what they needed for the day. He told them not to put any away past the day. They had to discipline themselves to live by faith. Not knowing where the manna was coming from, or when it would stop, they were to trust God that it was going to keep coming day by day. This discipline would prepare them to trust God when there was abundance, to do whatever He told them to do with their resources and know that He would continue to meet their need. This discipline would have them in position to obey and hear God with the abundance in the promised land, flowing with milk and honey, just as they did when they just kept back enough for the day in the wilderness.

Daily Bread Living *is living by every word that proceeds out of the mouth of God (Matt 4:4), in order that we may handle life's resources, circumstances, and obstacles with the mind of God.*

Man shall not live by bread alone but by every word that proceeds out of the mouth of God (Deut. 8:1-3; Matthew 4:4; Luke 4:4).

There are three particular meanings that are expressed here by God, that when we understand and implement them into our minds and hearts our lives will transition from our wilderness seasons of processing, into our promise land season of possessing. The Children of Israel were in the wilderness for 40 years being processed to possess their promise, but never possessed it because they never yielded to the processing.

They never learned the truth from this statement from God of how to live once you get to your promise land. But Jesus showed us that converse reality of learning from this truth and coming out of His wilderness temptations and PROCESSING to possess His promise in 40 DAYS. Which one will you choose? 40 DAYS in the wilderness of processing OR 40 YEARS?

Man Shall Not Live by Bread Alone

The first Meaning from these verses *MAN SHALL NOT LIVE BY BREAD ALONE IS ... Because you are not just a body, but you are a spirit that possesses a soul, who lives in a body...you cannot truly live by what you put in your body only.... but by the Word of God you put in your spirit also.*

If you feed your body food and do not feed your spirit the Word of God the real you, Your Spirit will die... So, the first meaning from these verses is *You cannot truly live by only feeding your body.*

The second meaning of this verse is that since you are not just a citizen in the earth as a natural man/woman...but also a citizen of Heaven; *"You cannot truly live by what see in this natural realm alone, but by what is seen in the heavenly realm by the eyes of faith through the word of God.*

Heb 11:1 Now faith is the substance of things hoped for, the evidence of things not seen.

And lastly, the third meaning of this verse that you are to understand and live by if you're ever going come out of your wilderness into your promised land is, *you cannot live by your job alone but by every word from your God.* <u>Your job is a resource, but your God is your source</u>.

If you try to only live by your resource you will never make it to the place or promise that God, your source, has for you. Man shall not live by His job alone (what He does for a living) But by every word of God (What He does for a giving...of his life). YOU WORK TO GIVE NOT TO LIVE...Eph 4:28

Let him that stole steal no more: but rather let him labor, working with his hands the thing which is good, that he may have to give to him that need. Ephesians 4:28

Notice I did NOT say you should not work. We were made to work that which will produce in both heaven and earth. (Gen 1:26-28). But you were not made to work DISCONNECTED from your time spent with GOD, the source of your work.

Daily Bread living is a spiritual, supernatural budgeting system from God from His word that prepares us to go through the wilderness of life through to the promises of God for our lives with wisdom and revelation to arrive to our destination with the mind of God, plan of God and purpose of God.

Budgeting is a vital part of increase and abundance. In Egypt, when Joseph was governor over the land, God gave him wisdom to store up a certain rate in the years of plenty, so that during the time of famine there would be enough food for everyone.

My Money Is Restored

In 1998 while I was reading the story of Joseph in Genesis the Lord gave me a word from Genesis 42:25-28 to begin confessing and possessing the wealth of the unrighteous from the world system. The phrase from Genesis 42:25 was; MY MONEY IS RESTORED.

Genesis 42:25-28 Then Joseph commanded to fill their sacks with corn, and to restore every man's money into his sack, and to give them provision for the way: and thus, did he unto them. And he laded their asses with corn and departed thence. And as one of them opened his sack to give his ass provender in the inn, he espied his money; for, behold, it was in his sack's mouth. And he said unto his brethren, "MY MONEY IS RESTORED; AND, LO IT IS EVEN IN MY SACK."

While reading the story of Joseph in scripture, in Genesis 41-46, and while studying the circumstances surrounding his rise to Prime Minister of Egypt, it dawned on me that when the world is in famine God not only wants to provide for his people, he wants to position his people to arise to a place of prominence and prosperity in the earth. It was during the time of the greatest famine the world had known that God had positioned one of His chosen people Joseph strategically in Egypt to preserve the sons of Jacob. And not only preserve them but prosper and release to them everything they would need to become a great and mighty people in that foreign nation.

This level of prayer deals with the aspect of the supernatural provision of God that God releases to His people as He's transitioning them from one realm to another, from Egypt to the promise land, from sin to righteousness, from the Kingdom of darkness to the Kingdom of God.

One of the signatures of the end-time revival of the provision and prosperity of God in His church will be the return of the church of Jesus Christ to living supernaturally, or by living by the miraculous provision and multiplication of the resources of God. We will begin to return to living by the supernatural power of God once again. We will begin to live by the supernatural provision of God once again, and we will live by the supernatural protection of God once again.

This will be a time of living more in the miraculous realm of God's provision, than living by conventional means, of a steady income from a 9 to 5 job. This will be a time of living, not on the world monetary system, nor on the economic system of this world, but on the economy of heaven. During the coming Day of the Lord, and the coming shaking of our world economic system, jobs will be scarce, food will be scarce, and the system will be corrupted and set-up to control the masses. With all the things that this shaking of the world system is going to bring to the earth, this is not the time to be living off of this world system. This is not the time to be living by conventional means, but above the system of this natural realm by supernatural means through a dependency upon God as they did in the wilderness when He rained down Manna from Heaven. In 1998, 3 years before the stock market crash of 2001, God gave me a dream and a revelation from Gen 42:28, to sustain His people in these times of economic collapse; "**MONEY IS RESTORED** - *How to Arise during the coming Financial Fall."*

This Word of wisdom is what we lived by both in 2001 and in 2008 when the economy fell. In May of 2008, 4 months before the housing collapse of Sept 2008 the Spirit of God spoke to me as I feel Him speaking now about 2019. He said, *"tell my people this is a time of living in the supernatural realm, or the spirit realm, not on the natural, not on the world system, or on the economy of this world, but on the economy of heaven."* He said, *it is time to live by every word that proceeds out of my mouth, by the word, and not by the world."* Below are the principles of supernatural living He gave me in 1998 from my book, My Money is Restored.

The 9 Principles of Supernatural Living

1. Supernatural living is living by what he has, not by what you have.

2. Supernatural living is living by every word (that proceeds out of the mouth of God) not by a word.

3. Supernatural living is living by prayer without ceasing, 24/7 day and night prayer for the release of Justice (Jesus).

4. Supernatural living is living by the spirit – *the gifts of the spirit*, (word of wisdom, word of knowledge, discerning of spirits, working of miracles, faith, gifts of healings, tongues, interpretation of tongues, and prophecy) not by the flesh.
5. Supernatural living is living a fasted lifestyle, fasting once or twice a week. (*7 days without fasting makes one weak*)

6. Supernatural living is living not just by his word, but by your word. (*Keeping your word to God and man, releases the word of the Lord from God to man*).

7. Supernatural natural living is living by loving, not by lusting.

8. Supernatural living is living in intimacy with the Lord, Loving the Lord your God with all of your heart, mind and soul. Not by head knowledge about the Lord, and just loving the things of God or the things from God.

9. Supernatural living is living by your giving, not by making a living.

INDIVIDUAL DECLARATIONS: MY MONEY IS RESTORED - Say this out Loud*: God is my Father. I am learning to depend totally on Him for my every need. Therefore, I have peace with God. God is my father. I am learning to give whatever He tells me to give. God is my business CEO, and I learn to trust His decisions. I consult Him about everything I do. This brings a peace that surpasses all understanding. I have faith into grace and peace with God. Therefore, my life, family, relationships, finances and businesses are abounding. I walk in the anointing of abundance.* **MY MONEY IS RESTORED!!!**

SAY THIS OUT LOUD: I am justified by the blood of Jesus. I am saved by faith; therefore, I live by faith. Because I am just, because I live by faith, the wealth of the sinner is being transferred into my hands.

I am a money magnet because I am a faith magnet. Money comes to me because I do whatever he tells me to do. I have the money I need for everything God tells me to do. When it comes, I handle it in faith. I am faithful to increase what God puts in my hands for the kingdom of God. My money grows because my faith and my faithfulness grows. My money is a tool. My money is a hook to win and attract the world to Christ. My money has a mission. My money has a vision. My money is called to win the World to Christ. The world is being saved and won to Christ because **MY MONEY IS RESTORED**

SAY THIS OUT LOUD: The tithe belongs to God. It connects my covenant with God, making whatever I have his and whatever he has mine. Through my tithe my money is being restored from the world to God to win the world to Christ. I have revelation knowledge on the right purpose of tithing. Therefore, I handle my resources with the mind of God. I am qualified to handle money in abundance. The anointing of restoration rest upon my life. **MY MONEY IS RESTORED!!!**

Today Pray in tongues for 30 minutes and meditate for 30 minutes on Ex 16:7; Matt. 4:4 Gen. 42:25-28, and confess the confessions below out loud, along with this 4th phrase from the Disciples Prayer: GIVE US THIS DAY OUR DAILY BREAD.

Scriptural Meditation for Give US this day Our Daily Bread

Exo 16:6 And Moses and Aaron said unto all the children of Israel, At even, then ye shall know that the LORD hath brought you out from the land of Egypt:

Exo 16:7 And in the morning, then ye shall see the glory of the LORD; for that he heareth your murmurings against the LORD: and what are we, that ye murmur against us?

Exo 16:8 And Moses said, This shall be, when the LORD shall give you in the evening flesh to eat, and in the morning bread to the full; for that the LORD heareth your murmurings which ye murmur against him: and what are we? your murmurings are not against us, but against the LORD.

Exo 16:9 And Moses spake unto Aaron, Say unto all the congregation of the children of Israel, Come near before the LORD: for he hath heard your murmurings.

Mat 4:4 But he answered and said, It is written, Man shall not live by bread alone, but by every word that proceeds out of the mouth of God.

Gen 42:25 Then Joseph commanded to fill their sacks with corn, and to restore every man's money into his sack, and to give them provision for the way: and thus did he unto them.

Gen 42:26 And they laded their asses with the corn, and departed thence.

Gen 42:27 And as one of them opened his sack to give his ass provender in the inn, he espied his money; for, behold, it was in his sack's mouth.

Gen 42:28 And he said unto his brethren, My money is restored; and, lo, it is even in my sack: and their heart failed them, and they were afraid, saying one to another, What is this that God hath done unto us?

CORPORATE DECLARATIONS: MY MONEY IS RESTORED - Say this out Loud*: God is our Father. We're learning to depend totally on Him for our every need. Therefore, we have peace with God. God is our father. We're learning to give whatever He tells us to give. God is our business CEO, and we're learning to trust His decisions. We* consult Him about everything we do. This brings a peace that surpasses all understanding. We have faith into grace and peace with God. Therefore, our lives, families, relationships, finances and businesses are abounding. We walk in the anointing of abundance. **OUR MONEY IS RESTORED!!!**

SAY THIS OUT LOUD: We are justified by the blood of Jesus. We are saved by faith; therefore, we live by faith. Because we are just, because we live by faith, the wealth of the sinner is being transferred into our hands. We are money magnets because we are faith magnets. Money comes to us because we do whatever He tells us to do. We have the money we need for everything God tells us to do. When it comes, we handle it in faith. We are faithful to increase what God puts our hands for the kingdom of God. Our money grows because our faith and my faithfulness grows. Our money is a tool. Our money is a hook to win and attract the world to Christ. Our money has a mission. Our money has a vision. Our money is called to win the World to Christ. The world is being saved and won to Christ because **OUR MONEY IS RESTORED**

SAY THIS OUT LOUD: The tithe belongs to God. It connects our covenant with God, making whatever we have His and whatever He has ours. Through our tithe our money is being restored from the world to God to win the world to Christ. We have revelation knowledge on the right purpose of tithing. Therefore, we handle our resources with the mind of God. We are qualified to handle money in abundance. The anointing of restoration rest upon my life. **OUR MONEY IS RESTORED!!!**

CHAPTER 10

(DAY 5) FORGIVE US OUR DEBTS AS WE FORGIVE OUR DEBTORS

–The Anointing of Healing and Reconciliation in Prayer

(Thursday Day 5) - Fast until 6pm and Pray in tongues for 30 minutes and Meditate for 30 minutes on Matt 10:6; Luke 17:15; and this 5th phrase from the disciple's prayer; FORGIVE US OUR DEBTS AS WE FORGIVE OUR DEBTORS)

TODAY'S MEDTITATION: The fifth dimension in prayer is The Earthly Realm of The Man's Dimension in prayer. "When you pray, say...*Forgive us our debts as we forgive our debtors*...This level of prayer deals with the aspect of having a heart of forgiveness so that we may keep ourselves free from diseases and sicknesses that come from the root of bitterness.

The Connection of Jesus' High Priestly Prayer with the Disciples Prayer

This phrase of the *Disciples Prayer* "<u>Forgive us our Debts as we forgive our Debtors</u>" connects with the High Priestly prayer of Jesus in John 17 at verse 21, which says, *"That they all may be one; as thou, Father, art in me, and I in thee, that they also may be one in us: that the world may believe that thou hast sent me."* Our

[handwritten note: all through the POWER of FORGIVENESS]

receiving forgiveness from God through Jesus Christ and our forgiving one another because of God's forgiveness of us by Jesus Christ, brings the answer and fulfillment of Jesus' prayer for us, that we would be *one,* as the Father is in Christ and Christ is in the Father and we all are in both the Father and the Son, through the power of the Holy Ghost, all through forgiveness.

Matthew 6:14, 15 tells us if we don't forgive our brother of his trespasses, our Heavenly father will not forgive us of our trespasses.

Forgiveness is the key to deliverance. Many born-again believers still struggle with iniquitous sin patterns and generational curses that they're unable to get free from because of unforgiveness. If we don't send away the sins of those that have trespassed against us, our Father in heaven can't send away our sins. Forgiveness is a combination of two words; "Fore" which means forward, or to go before or ahead of, and "Give" which means to offer up or send away. From this etymological word breakdown of forgiveness, we can see that forgiveness actually means; to give ahead of the offence. Forgiveness means; to give or offer reconciliation in the Love of God, before the offense to cover the offense. *Above all, keep fervent in your love for one another, because love covers a multitude of sins. 1 Peter 4:8.*

Another reason we're unable to get free from patterns, cycles and generational curses of sin is because we don't really understand forgiveness. We don't truly understand what it means to be forgiven. We think our forgiveness is based on something we do, like confession of every one of the sins we commit in order to be forgiven. However, forgiveness is not based on something we do, nor anything we can do. It's based on what Jesus did on the cross two thousand years ago.

Col 2:13 And you, being dead in your sins and the uncircumcision of your flesh, hath he quickened together with him, **_having forgiven_**

you all trespasses; *14 Blotting out the handwriting of ordinances that was against us, which was contrary to us, and **took it out of the way, nailing it to his cross**;*

Paul tells us that we have been forgiven of ALL of our sins. That's not just the sins you committed in your past before you came to Christ. That's all of your past sins, present sins you may be in right now, and all of the future sins you may commit in your future. YOU ARE FORGIVEN! You are not going to be forgiven of your sins, you ARE forgiven of your sins. Many misunderstand forgiveness and confession, and as a result we spend our Christian lives trying to do inventory of sins that we've committed, trying to chase down everything we've ever done to assure that our lives are sinless and that the sins we've committed are forgiven. This is the wrong theological concept of forgiveness. Confession is not something you do for all the sins that you commit, confession is something you do for all the things that Christ say's is sin. Confession is agreeing with Christ that those things that you do that are called sin by Him, are called sin by you, not your problem, your issue, or struggle. No! it's not just your struggle, it's your sin. Confession is agreeing with what God says about sin. Whatever you call sin, in agreement with what God calls sin, you've been forgiven of it. If it's sin, you've been forgiven of it. If He calls it sin and you don't, you can't be forgiven of it. You can't be forgiven of sin you are unwilling to acknowledge is sin, once He reveals it clearly to you as sin.

1Jn 1:9 If we confess our sins, he is faithful and just to forgive us our sins, and to cleanse us from all unrighteousness.

Whatever we confess as sin, is forgiven. When the prayer says, *forgive us our debts as we forgive our debtors*, it's talking about more than our present sins, it's talking about all the sins of our generations, our generational sins that have added up, piled up and have raised a wall and put stumbling blocks between us and our purpose, between us and our original person, or callings, or between us and our wilderness journey, transference and transition from the Egypt of the sinful world we live in, through the wilderness of our transformation, to the destination of our promised land. The Holy Spirit for the believer is comparable to the cloud by day, and fire by night for the children of Israel in the wilderness. As God led them through the wilderness through all their enemies, both within and without, a revelation of forgiveness confronts the enemies of fear, lust, sexual perversion, lack or the like, that may be standing between you and your promised land. As you Pray and Say, *"Forgive our debts as we forgive our debtors,"* we overcome every one of our enemies from our past, present or future, assuring we won't ever go back to Egypt, but complete our journey to our promised land in the kingdom of God.

How Do We Forgive

The nature of God as a God of Love is wrapped up in the meaning of forgiveness. It means to suffer wrong to make right. Love is giving at the expense of self. Lust is taking at the expense of another.

Forgiveness is a by-product of the Love of God, without which there can be no forgiveness. To walk in forgiveness, you not only must walk in Love, but you must walk in faith. Faith works by love.

Luke 17:3-6 Be on your guard! If your brother sins, rebuke him; and if he repents, forgive him. 4. And if he sins against you seven times a day, and returns to you seven times, saying, 'I repent,' forgive him."5. The apostles said to the Lord, "Increase our faith!" 6. And the Lord said, "If you had faith like a mustard seed, you would say to this mulberry tree, 'Be uprooted and be planted in the sea'; and it would obey you.

To walk in Faith to forgive ahead of the offense we must put the word of Faith in our hearts ahead of the offense. We must sow faith for forgiveness through the foresight of verse 1 of Luke 17 that says; 1. *Then said he unto the disciples, it is impossible but that offenses will come.* With the knowledge that we're going to encounter offenses in relationships, we must build ourselves up on our most holy faith so that our faith is capable of seeing people as God sees them and forgive them because God has forgiven both them and you.

We must learn to forgive not looking for an apology or reparations from those who offended us. This is what Jesus did for us on Calvary. Before we even knew we were sinners He forgave us of our sins, not looking to be repaid for what was done to him. This is how we are to forgive. We are to forgive before anyone ever apologizes for an offence, not to warrant an apology but because we don't need apology.

Africans/African Americans in Christ Should need no Apology to Forgive

When we actually know what God was doing in us and for us, as well as what God wanted to take us to, through all of the oppression, slavery and discrimination, we will no longer need or want anyone to apologize to us for their actions, or their ancestors' actions. One day when we understand what our plight was all about and why we went through what we went through, we will have the response of Joseph when his brothers wanted to apologize to him for selling him into slavery in Egypt in the book of Genesis 50:15-20. The account goes like this;

> *15. And when Joseph's brethren saw that their father was dead, they said Joseph will peradventure hate us, and will certainly requite us all the evil which we did unto him. 16. And they sent a messenger unto*

Joseph, saying, Thy Father did command before he died, saying,

17. So shall ye say unto Joseph, FORGIVE, I PRAY THEE NOW, THE TRESPASS OF THY BRETHREN, AND THEIR SIN; FOR THEY DID UNTO THEE EVIL: and now, we pray thee, forgive the trespass of the servants of the God of thy father. And Joseph wept when they spoke unto him. 18. And his brethren also went and fell down before his face; and they said, Behold, we be thy servants.

19. AND JOSEPH SAID UNTO THEM, FEAR NOT: FOR AM I IN THE PLACE OF GOD? (Am I not where God wanted me?) 20. BUT AS FOR YOU, YOU THOUGHT EVIL AGAINST ME; BUT GOD MEANT IT UNTO GOOD, TO BRING TO PASS, AS IT IS THIS DAY, TO SAVE MUCH PEOPLE ALIVE.

21. Now therefore fear ye not: I will nourish you and your little ones. And he comforted them and spoke kindly unto them.

Joseph's brothers felt that Joseph would treat them wrongly after their father died for what they had done in selling him into slavery. So, Joseph's brothers sent messengers to Joseph, saying our father commanded before he died, saying *FORGIVE THE TRESPASS OF THY BRETHREN AND THEIR SIN;* I believe this represents to the African Diaspora world-wide as well as to all those that have ever been offended by their brethren from other races, how God expects us to respond to interracial offence. Our father, which art in Heaven said, to pray like this before he died; *Forgive us our trespasses as we forgive those that trespass against us*. This is what Jesus taught his disciples to pray before he died. Joseph's response is how the African Diaspora will one day respond, both to our African brothers who sold us into slavery and to our former oppressors who enslaved us. When we see what God was doing in us and for us, through our being sold into slavery by our brothers, we will respond different to the experience. He said to his brothers, *AM I NOT IN THE PLACE GOD WANTED ME?* God was trying to get some of us out of Africa, into the nations of the world to bring reconciliation, deliverance and fullness and redeem and restore both Africa, America and Europe to the blessing and prosperity of God and man. We will one day be able to say as Joseph; *YOU THOUGHT EVIL AGAINST ME; BUT GOD MEANT IT UNTO GOOD, TO BRING TO PASS, AS IT IS THIS DAY TO SAVE MUCH PEOPLE ALIVE*.

When we understand that our slavery was a positioning for us to be deliverers both to our brothers (our race) and to other nations (races), we will no longer need or want to accept apologies for what we've been through. God was doing more through our slavery and oppression, like Joseph, to position us in the nations of the world for reconciliation and the saving of the nations.

Psa. 105:17 He sent a man before them, **even Joseph, who was sold for a slave:** *18 Whose feet they hurt with fetters: he was laid in iron: 19* <u>Until the time that his word came: the word of the LORD tried him.</u>

Just like Joseph was sent through slavery into Africa to redeem his brothers that came to him from Canaan during the famine, Africans were later sent by God, through slavery into the America's, Caribbean's and Europe, to save a generation at the end of the age, during the coming time of the tribulation, as we transition from the kingdoms of this world to the Kingdom of God. And just Like Joseph, Jesus doesn't want, nor will He accept our apologies for our sins nailing him to the cross. Jesus wants our reconciliation to God and to one another. The cross was how the enemy of this life, Satan, would be defeated, and our sins would be eradicated, setting us free from sins' payday of destruction and death. This is what Jesus did for us on Calvary. So, ought we to do likewise to our fellowman. Jesus further teaches us how to forgive in Luke 17:4, 5 When the disciples were distraught about how they were to forgive as many times as your brother needs it, Peter said, Lord Increase our Faith.

How Do We Build Up Ourselves in The Faith?

How do we build up ourselves in the faith to forgive, not yet seeing the purpose of our affliction or oppression in past generations? We do so by meditating on the word of Faith and by praying in the Holy Ghost (tongues). Faith comes by hearing the Word (Rom. 10:17) So, faith for forgiveness comes by hearing the word of forgiveness. Also, praying in tongues builds our faith up to stay in Love and release forgiveness when people offend us.

But you, beloved, building yourselves up on your most holy faith, praying in the Holy Spirit, 21. keeping yourselves in the love of God, waiting anxiously for the mercy of our Lord Jesus Christ to eternal life.

Forgiveness Is Given by Faith

Sowing the seed of the Word of God on forgiveness puts faith for forgiveness in your heart. Prayer in the Holy Ghost builds up your faith. Faith in your heart that is growing by the Spirit is what produces the fruit of the spirit to forgive when someone offends you. But you can't wait until someone offends you to put the faith for forgiveness in your heart. You must put it there before the storm of offense comes, in order to have the faith to forgive when the offenses come. This is why we need a regular day to pray this phrase and meditate on **"Forgive us our Debts as we Forgive our Debtors,"** because if you're not regularly praying meditating and confessing your need to forgive you could be blindsided when the offense comes, and you don't have forgiveness in your heart to forgive. If you are living by your feelings and not by faith in God's word when the offense comes your relationships will suffer fatalities that you may never recover from. And the root of bitterness that comes from the offense could end up working its way up one day from the surface into your flesh, resulting in incurable diseases, and sexually immoral practices that end in divorce of your marriage, or the cutting off of a covenant relationship, that could spell the destruction of your life and destiny. The root cause of most diseases are bitterness and offense that have not been dealt with at the heart, root level. This causes us to live controlled by our carnal, selfish, sinful nature. And a carnal man living controlled by his feelings will never be able to forgive because his feelings will always get in the way of what God's word is saying. And this carnality ends in death.

Scriptural Meditations for Resolving Conflicts and Making Godly Appeals

Jesus prayed earnestly in John 17 that His people would walk in unity through forgiveness. This reveals how much He values it. He also gave us how to resolve conflicts and make Godly appeals.

Below are some verses to help you as you meditate today on: FORGIVE US OUR DEBTS AS WE FORGIVE OUR DEBTORS

Mat 18:15 Moreover if thy brother shall trespass against thee, go and tell him his fault between thee and him alone: if he shall hear thee, thou hast gained thy brother.

Mat 18:16 But if he will not hear thee, then take with thee one or two more, that in the mouth of two or three witnesses every word may be established.

Mat 18:17 And if he shall neglect to hear them, tell it unto the church: but if he neglects to hear the church, let him be unto thee as a heathen man and a publican.

Mat 18:18 Verily I say unto you, Whatsoever ye shall bind on earth shall be bound in heaven: and whatsoever ye shall loose on earth shall be loosed in heaven.

Mat 18:19 Again I say unto you, that if two of you shall agree on earth as touching anything that they shall ask, it shall be done for them of my Father which is in heaven.

That they all may be one...23 that they may be made perfect in one... (Jn. 17:21-23)

Restoring Wounded Relationships

The spirit of a relationship can be wounded (without the people themselves being wounded). In other words, when former trust and communication are injured, then the relationship is wounded. A relationship can be wounded long before it is broken. A broken relationship requires much more skill and attention to heal. If we address the relational wounds or infection at the early stages, then we can avoid divisiveness in the body and "gangrene" that kills the relationship. As a spiritual family, we seek to repair slightly wounded relationships before they become broken relationships. It is better to be proactive—an ounce of prevention is worth a pound of cure.

It is difficult to win an offended brother back to an open spirit (an easy flowing relationship). The purpose of a fortified city is to keep certain people out of it.

19 A brother offended is harder to win than a strong city... (Prov. 18:19)

19 An offended brother is more unyielding [unresponsive] than a fortified city... (Prov. 18:19 NIV)

The primary cause of a wounded relationship is the sense of not being wanted (feeling rejected). The signs of a wounded relationship include a sense of not being wanted, a guarded heart (less receptive and more cautious), and strained communication (a defensive tone).

18 There is no fear [of rejection] in love; but perfect love casts out fear, because fear involves torment [fear of being judged]. He who fears has not been made perfect in love. (1 Jn. 4:18)

Making A Godly Appeal

When any feel mistreated in our ministry infrastructures, they should make an appeal first to the Lord, then to the brother who mistreated them, and then to the leaders who have authority to help with the solution. To share an offense with a friend who is not a part of the solution is slander.

15 If your brother sins against you, go and tell him his fault between you and him alone...

16 But if he will not hear, take with you one or two more... (Mt. 18:15-16)

Tell him his fault: Some appeals to a brother can start in an email or phone call, but most will require a face-to-face meeting. When we meet face to face, we feel differently. Often the Spirit will intervene, and we will feel more affection and mercy than when talking about him to others. Many do not meet with their brother to save time. (It usually costs much more time by not meeting). We are changed by the process of gaining courage and clarity in appealing to our brother. We often discover much about our heart and weakness in the process of preparing to appeal to our brother. If we skip this step, we lose opportunity for growth and for our brother to respond to us.

1 If a man is overtaken in any trespass...restore such a one in a spirit of gentleness, considering yourself lest you also be tempted. 2 Bear one another's burdens... (Gal. 6:1-2)

The leaders are required to be strictly confidential (unless bringing in leaders over them to help).

A talebearer reveals secrets...he who is of a faithful spirit conceals a matter. (Prov. 11:13)

Making the Appeal

Our appeal starts with asking questions, requesting help, and sharing feelings first to the Lord and then to the brother. If needed, we then go to a leader in a position to help with the solution.

First, we appeal to the Lord.

> 1. Ask questions of the Lord: Before meeting, we ask the Lord what He thinks about them and the conflict. We ask Him to speak into our deficiencies in the conflict and how we lacked sensitivity in the

> relationship. We use this to humble ourselves before our brother.
> 2. **Request help from the Lord:** Ask Him to prepare the heart of the brother (spouse, child, etc.) before your meeting. The Lord may give a prophetic dream or speak to their heart.
> 3. **Share your feelings with the Lord:** about the brother, the conflict, and relationship. This helps us to get in touch with our positive and negative feelings that are pent up inside us.

Second, we begin our appeal to the brother by asking questions, making requests, and sharing. This gives us opportunity to gain insight into blind spots in our heart and to understand his heart better. It is not effective to start the meeting with accusations or seeking to win an argument.

> 1. **Ask questions of the brother:** instead of starting the meeting with statements against the brother. For example, "What were you thinking when you told me...?"
> 2. **Request help from the brother:** Ask him for help to understand his heart. For example, "Help me process or understand what I heard or was feeling when you told me..."
> 3. **Share your feeling with the brother:** We share how we feel or what we heard him say, instead of making accusations. For example, "I felt rejected when you said..." or "I heard you saying that you wanted me off the team when you said..."

We must confess our faults to our brother. Do not say, "I am sorry, if I have offended you," but say, "I repent of sinning against you," (by coming up short in love). When we say that we are sorry if they were offended, we are actually saying that they are easily offended, and we are not really saying sorry at all.

16 Confess your trespasses to one another, and pray for one another, that you may be healed (Jas. 5:16)

We Must Judge with the Right Spirit

Jesus commanded us to rebuke a brother who sins against us and to use righteous judgments. Scripture commands the Church to bring righteous judgment to those with destructive doctrines and behavior (Mt. 18:15-17; 1 Cor. 5:1-11; 2 Cor. 11:12-15; Eph. 5:11; 1 Thes. 5:14, 21; 2 Thes. 3:6-14; 1 Tim. 5:19-20; 2 Tim. 4:2; Titus 1:10-13; 2:15; 3:10-11; 1 Jn. 4:1; Rev. 2:2, 14-15, 20).

3 If your brother sins against you, rebuke him; and if he repents, forgive him. (Lk. 17:3)

24 Do not judge according to appearance, but judge with righteous judgment. (Jn. 7:24)

Many misinterpret this verse to mean we must never say that someone is wrong. The word judge means to analyze or evaluate, to approve or condemn, with the intention of making wrong things right. We must do it in the right process for the right purpose and with the right spirit. This requires a "vigorous spirituality" to invest the time and humility to discern all the real issues.

1 Judge not, that you be not judged. 2 For with what judgment you judge, you will be judged; and with the measure you use, it will be measured back to you...5 First remove the plank from your eye, and you will see clearly to remove the speck out of your brother's eye. (Mt. 7:1-5)

Gently: We approach them tenderly without harshness as we hope for the best in the process. We look for their sincere intention to obey Jesus, and we confess some of our struggles to them.

1 If a man is overtaken in any trespass, you who are spiritual restore such a one in a spirit of gentleness, considering yourself lest you also be tempted. (Gal. 6:1)

1 A soft answer turns away wrath [anger], but a harsh word stirs up anger. (Prov. 15:1)

Humbly: We are to examine ourselves because the knowledge of our own failures humbles us. We are to approach others with a sense of our personal failure and take responsibility for our faults. We should seek to repent quickly, with a teachable spirit that is able to "hear," without being defensive.

5 First remove the plank from your own eye, and then you will see clearly to remove the speck out of your brother's eye. (Mt. 7:5)

Accurately: We take time and effort to get all the available information. Those content with partial information have already made up their minds against another. We do not know all the complex details in the circumstances of another's life.

13 He who answers a matter before he hears it, it is folly and shame to him...17 The first one to plead his cause seems right, until his neighbor...examines him. (Prov. 18:13 17)

19 Let every man be swift to hear, slow to speak, slow to wrath. (Jas. 1:19)

Patiently: We give people time to understand the gravity of their sin, and time to repent, without quickly concluding that they refuse to repent. We must not rush through the process too quickly.

21 I gave her (Jezebel) time to repent of her sexual immorality... (Rev. 2:21)

Confidentiality: We only make the information known to those with authority to help in the restoration process. We do not reveal the past sins of anyone who repents.

13 A talebearer reveals secrets, but he who is of a faithful spirit conceals a matter. (Prov. 11:13)

8 Above all things have fervent love...for love will cover a multitude of sins. (1 Pet. 4:8)

9 He who covers a transgression seeks love, but he who repeats a matter separates friends. (Prov. 17:9)

Mercy is more successful than judgment. We seek to show mercy by not requiring that they appeal with 100% accuracy in their facts against us. If only 5% is accurate, then focus on that 5% and ask their forgiveness for it. Try to hear their pain and to understand how we contributed to it.

13 Mercy triumphs over judgment. (Jas. 2:13)

The Spirit is the guardian of the culture of the Body of Christ. He requires that we dwell together in a culture of honor. Blessing comes from honor. Honor heals and dishonor divides. We seek to see their budding virtues that we may bless them. To be of the same mind requires that we seek to be agreeable instead of resistant. We seek to "get on their team." Do not be wise in your opinion; in other words, do not presume to understand all that God sees in them and the conflict.

10 In honor giving preference to one another...14 bless and do not curse...16 Be of the same mind toward one another...Do not be wise in your own opinion...18 as much as depends on you, live peaceably with all men... (Rom. 12:10-18)

TODAY'S INDIVDUAL PRAYER DECLARATION *I declare today that I am forgiven by the blood of Jesus. My sins and transgressions have been nailed to the cross. I am forgiven of all of my sins, past, present and future in Jesus name. Nothing can separate me from the love of god which is in Christ Jesus. Not tribulation, or distress, not persecution, or famine, not nakedness, peril, or sword. Nothing can separate me from the love of Christ. Because I am forgiven, and because his blood has cleansed me from all of my sins, I forgive all those who have sinned against me. I release all those that have offended me. I forgive and release my spouse, my parents, my children, and close friends. I release all bitterness. I release all unforgiveness. And I pray for those that have persecuted me and bless those that have tried to curse me. My forgiveness of all my iniquities releases salvation, healing, debt free living and prosperity into my life in Jesus name. My forgiveness of all my iniquities breaks every generational curse of sickness, disease, malady or malfunction over my life. My forgiveness of all my iniquities releases worship and the love for god and man into my life in Jesus' name.*

(Thursday Day 5) - Fast until 6pm and Pray in tongues for 30 minutes and Meditate for 30 minutes on Matt 10:6; Luke 17:15; and this 5th phrase from the disciple's prayer; FORGIVE US OUR DEBTS AS WE FORGIVE OUR DEBTORS)

Scriptural Mediation for Forgive Us Debts as we Forgive Our Debtors

Mat 6:14 For if ye forgive men their trespasses, your heavenly Father will also forgive you: 15 But if ye forgive not men their trespasses, neither will your Father forgive your trespasses.

Luk 17:1 Then said he unto the disciples, It is impossible but that offences will come: but woe unto him, through whom they come!

Luk 17:2 It were better for him that a millstone were hanged about his neck, and he cast into the sea, than that he should offend one of these little ones. Luk 17:3 Take heed to yourselves: If thy brother trespass against thee, rebuke him; and if he repent, forgive him.

Luk 17:4 And if he trespass against thee seven times in a day, and seven times in a day turn again to thee, saying, I repent; thou shalt forgive him.

Luk 17:5 And the apostles said unto the Lord, Increase our faith.

Luk 17:6 And the Lord said, If ye had faith as a grain of mustard seed, ye might say unto this sycamine tree, Be thou plucked up by the root, and be thou planted in the sea; and it should obey you.

TODAY'S CORPORATE PRAYER DECLARATION: *We declare today that we are forgiven by the blood of Jesus. Our sins and transgressions have been nailed to the cross. We are forgiven of all of our sins, past, present and future in Jesus name. Nothing can separate us from the love of God which is in Christ Jesus. Not tribulation, or distress, not persecution, or famine, not nakedness, peril, or sword. Nothing can separate us from the love of Christ. Because we are forgiven, and because his blood has cleansed us from all of our sins, we forgive all those who have sinned against us. We release all those that have offended us. We forgive and release spouses, parents, children, close friends. We release all bitterness. We release all unforgiveness. And we pray for those that have persecuted us and bless those that have tried to curse us. Our forgiveness of all our iniquities releases salvation, healing, debt free living and prosperity into our lives, in Jesus name. Our forgiveness of all our iniquities breaks every generational curse of sickness, disease, malady or malfunction off our lives. Our forgiveness of all our iniquities releases worship and the love for god and man into our lives in Jesus name.*

CHAPTER 11

(DAY 6) LEAD US NOT INTO TEMPTATION BUT DELIVER US FROM EVIL (THE EVIL ONE) –

The Deliverance Anointing for Overcoming the Spirit of Jezebel

(Friday Day 6) - Today Pray in tongues for at least 30 minutes and meditate on Gen. 3:1-6 Joel 2:32; Obadiah 1:17, 18; Luke 4:18, 19; Ephesians 6:10-22; Rev 2:18-22; I Cor. 10:13 I Cor. 15:1, along with this 6th phrase from the Disciples Prayer: <u>Lead us not into the Temptation but Deliver us From Evil.</u>

TODAY'S MEDITATION: The next (6th) dimension in the disciple's prayer is **the Kingdom realm of the deliverance dimension** in prayer, accessing deliverance from one kingdom to another, for victory over the principalities of the kingdom of darkness. Jesus said **WHEN YOU PRAY, SAY**...*LEAD US NOT INTO TEMPTATION BUT DELIVER US FROM EVIL (ONE)...*

The Connection of Jesus' High Priestly Prayer with the Disciples Prayer

This phrase of the *Disciples Prayer* <u>*"Lead us not into temptation but deliver us from evil*</u> connects with Jesus' high priestly prayer in John 17 at verse 15; *I do not ask You to take them out of the world, but to Keep Them from The Evil One.* This level of prayer deals with the aspect of being kept from the evil one until we're equipped to resist his temptations and his seductive power to kill, steal and destroy us. Satan attempts to destroy us through the deceptive practices of the principalities of Jezebel, to lead us astray into a perversion and imitation of the kingdom of God, in the kingdom of darkness.

Lead Us Not into Temptation (Seduction)

To be kept from temptation is to be kept from being seduced by the spirit of the world that manifests through various cunning, crafty spirits that attempt to deceive us and get us off course from the path God has laid out for us in Christ. However, this 6th phrase of the disciple's prayer that speaks of not being led into temptation but being delivered from evil, is speaking of God not allowing the evil one in the evil day to come upon us UNTIL we are strong enough in the LORD and in the power of HIS might. This phrase is speaking of the believer being empowered to stand against him, having the power to resist the attacks of the enemy in the evil day, so that we may be DELIVERED into kingdom power and glory at the Lord's return.

ARMOR UP to Stand against the Wiles of the Devil

Think about it for a moment, if the prayer was just talking about not being tempted at all, then there would be no need for I Corinthians 10:12, 13

1Co 10:12 Wherefore let him that thinketh he stands take heed lest *he fall. 13 There hath no temptation taken you but such as is common to man: but God is faithful, who will not suffer you to be tempted above that ye are able; <u>but will with the temptation also make a way to escape,</u> that ye may be able to bear it.*

Furthermore, if this prayer phrase, "*Lead us not into temptation*" was about being kept from temptation entirely, then Luke 4:1 and Matthew 4 that speaks of the Spirit leading Jesus into the wilderness to be tempted of the devil would contradict this prayer.

Luk 4:1 And Jesus being full of the Holy Ghost returned from Jordan, <u>and was led by the Spirit into the wilderness, 2 Being forty days tempted of the devil</u>.

Mat 4:1 Then was Jesus **<u>led up of the Spirit into the wilderness to be tempted of the devil.</u>**

This phrase is mostly speaking of not being led into your season, or day of temptation with evil and the evil one UNTIL, like Jesus in Luke 4:1, you are FULL of the Holy Ghost. The enemy wants to catch us off guard and unprepared without our whole armor on as is depicted in Ephesians 6:18-21

Eph 6:10 Finally, my brethren, (1) **<u>be strong in the Lord, and in the power of his might.</u>** *11 Put on the whole armor of God, that ye may be able to stand against the wiles of the devil……*

13 Wherefore **<u>take unto you the whole armor of God</u>**, *that ye may be able to withstand in the evil day, and having done all, to stand. 14 Stand therefore, (2)* **<u>having your loins girt about with truth</u>**, *and having on (3)* **<u>the breastplate of righteousness</u>**;

15 And your(4) **<u>feet shod with the preparation of the gospel of peace;</u>** *16 Above all, (5)* **<u>taking the shield of faith</u>**, *wherewith ye* shall be able to quench all the fiery darts of the wicked. 17 And take (6) **the helmet of salvation**, and (7) **the sword of the Spirit, which is the word of God:**

Lead us not into temptation but deliver us from evil is speaking mainly of us not being taken into that evil day, both in our own individual lives, and at the end of the age, at the revealing of the Man of Sin, until we are ARMORED UP with the whole armor of God, that we are able to STAND against the wiles of the devil in that day, called the *Evil Day*.

The Spirit of Might – Be Strong in the Lord and in the Power of His Might

When we receive the spirit of God we must be built up by the spirit on our most Holy Faith, praying in the Holy Ghost (Jude 20) in order to be *strong in the Lord and in the power of His might (Ephesians 6:10),* which is the first article of the Armor of God...*The Spirit of Might* (Isaiah 11:2). This spirit enables us to be strong in our inner man, to be able to have faith, to hear and obey the counsel of the Lord, that leads us into God's wisdom that combats the principalities and powers of Satan in a region, or over a people group.

Eph 3:10 so that **the manifold wisdom of God** *might now* **be made known through the church to the rulers and the principalities** *in the heavenly places.*

Eph 6:10 Finally, my brethren, be strong in the Lord, and in the power of his might. 11 Put on the whole armor of God, that ye may be able to stand against the wiles of the devil.

Isa 11:2 And the spirit of the LORD shall rest upon him, the spirit of wisdom and understanding, **the spirit of counsel and might**, *the spirit of knowledge and of the fear of the LORD;*

The Spirit of Might is one of the seven Spirits of God and it is connected and teamed up in Isaiah 11:2 with the Spirit of Counsel...*The Spirit of Counsel and of Might.*

The Loin Belt of Truth: The next article of the armor of God we must put on is the *Loin belt of Truth*...And it is the truth or revelation of who Jesus is in this warfare against the enemy.... He's the Lion of the tribe of Judah. He is the captain of the Lord of Hosts. He is our Jehovah Nissi...The Lord our victory, who has already given us the victory over every demonic foe and attack of the enemy.

The Breastplate of Righteousness: The next armor we must put on before we go into our day of temptation is the breastplate of righteousness...And it is the armor that guards our heart against condemnation from the wicked one because of sin and the sin nature. Righteousness gives us the assurance that NO WEAPON formed against us shall prosper and every tongue that rises against us in judgment we shall condemn. (Isa. 54:17) How? Because Isaiah 54:17,18 says, this is our inheritance as servants of the Lord and OUR RIGHTEOUSNESS IS FROM HIM (JESUS CHRIST). Yes, we are the Righteousness of God in Christ. Therefore, we are not condemned to death when we sin.

There is therefore now no condemnation to them which are in Christ Jesus - Romans 8:1

Feet Shod with the Preparation of the Gospel of Peace: The next armor we must put on before we face our enemy in the evil day is the *armor of peace*...Having our feet shod with the preparation of the gospel of peace. Peace is the message of reconciliation. It's the message that we have been reconciled to God through Jesus Christ and have been made NEW. This message is a weapon, that when we go and tell what Jesus has done for us, we will defeat the enemies of death – separation, strife, division, and racism, both within the body of Christ and in the world.

The Shield of Faith: The next armor we must put on before we face our enemy in the evil day is the armor of *the Shield of Faith*. This is the part of the armor that requires us filling ourselves up with the word of God so that we are able to ward off all the fiery darts of the enemy when he comes to speak lies to us about us, our situation and our brothers and sisters in Christ. Faith comes by Hearing and Hearing by the word of God.

The Helmet of Salvation: The next armor we must put on before we face the enemy in the evil day is the armor of *the Helmet of Salvation*, which is the armor that protects our minds, and gives us knowledge of His will concerning what God has done for us in Jesus. We are saved from sin, from our spiritual and natural enemies, we are saved from the wrath to come and ultimately, we are saved from the power of death, hell and the grave.

The Sword of the Spirit which is the Word of God, with all prayer and petition in the Spirit: The final piece of the armor we must put on is the *Sword of the Spirit, which is the word of God, and all prayer and petition, prayer in the spirit at all times and on behalf of our leaders*. The final piece of the armor is often separated or stated incomplete by bible expositors and theologians. It's actually stated in scripture as *The Sword of the Spirit which is the Word of God, with all prayer and petition in the Spirit*. Most people refer to it only as the Sword of the Spirit. But this article is the only offensive piece of the armor and it connects the word of God and prayer together to defeat the enemy in your evil day, as Jesus did when He went into the wilderness to be tempted of the devil.

Jesus said *It Is Written* to the devil. He was opposing the devil in His secret time of prayer as the devil attempted to seduce Him into compromising His destiny with the lust of the eyes, the Lust of the flesh and the pride of Life. It's not until you face the devil in your private time with the word of God in prayer and are prepared to wield that sword of the word against the devil in your personal life and time alone, will you be prepared to take him on in the lives of others when you come out of your wilderness into your public calling and destiny in God. Therefore, we must *NOT* be willing to go into what God has called us to do, be or have until we are delivered from the enemy within us. We must be willing to pray; *Lead us not into the time of our temptation to compromise with a perversion of power, prestige and pleasure* UNTIL you've empowered us to be *delivered from this temptation in our evil day*. The evil day ultimately in the earth is that day of Great Tribulation and testing of God's people in the earth right before we come into all that God has promised us in the coming kingdom of God in the earth.

...and that we must **through much tribulation enter into the kingdom of God.** *(Acts 14:22)*

*...**Immediately after the tribulation of those days** .... shall appear the sign of the Son of man in heaven: and then shall all the tribes of the earth mourn, and they shall see the Son of man coming in the clouds of heaven with power and great glory. (Matt 24:29, 30)*
Because Jesus was full of the power of the spirit before He went into the wilderness to be tempted of the devil, He was able to resist the devil with the word of God, saying;

4 **And Jesus answered him**, saying, **It is written,** That man shall not live by bread alone, but by every word of God.

5 **And the devil, taking him up into an high mountain**, shewed unto him all the kingdoms of the world in a moment of time.

8 **And Jesus answered** and said unto him, Get thee behind me, Satan: **for it is written**, Thou shalt worship the Lord thy God, and him only shalt thou serve. Luke 4:4-8.

Standing against the Wiles of the Jezebel Spirit.

When Ephesians 6:10 tells us to be strong in the Lord and to put on the whole Armor of God...It's so that we may be able to stand firm against the schemes of the devil. It goes on to tell us that *we are not wrestling against flesh and blood, but against the rulers of darkness, and against the powers, against the world forces of this darkness against spirit forces of wickedness in the heavenly places*. One such principality and seducing scheme that the enemy manifests to seduce us into evil, to lead us astray, is the *spirit of Jezebel*. This is the main ruling spirit that attempts to lead us out of the kingdom of God and into the Kingdom of darkness. Therefore, we are directed to pray; **LEAD US NOT INTO TEMPTATION (SEDUCTION)**

The most important characteristic of the Jezebel spirit is that it's a spirit of seduction and perversion of what's right, which operates through sorcery to influence humanity away from God and His purpose of humanity made in the image of God. Or to influence humanity away from God's purpose for human sexuality of a man to a woman, or for the overall purpose for mankind after the original purpose and plan of God overall. The Jezebel Spirit is a ruling spirit in the earth set against the Spirit of God, set against the will of God and set against the purposes of God for mankind in the earth. The Jezebel spirit is a spirit that sets out to pervert the image of God in humanity and replace this image with an image of someone or something less than what God originally created for man to be or have.

Jezebel in the Old Testament

The woman Jezebel was an Old Testament personality that was the daughter of a pagan King, Ethbaal, King of the Sidonians, which married King Ahab, king of the nation of Israel, and influenced Israel from the worship of Jehovah to the worship of Baal, the god of the Sidonians. This woman, Jezebel is mentioned both in the Old Testament and the New Testament. However, Jezebel in the Old

Testament and Jezebel in the New Testament were two completely different ladies, but they operated in the same spirit - *the spirit of perversion and sorcery.* Her spirit was exhilarated by perversion, position, and power or prestige.

Definition of Perversion: *1a. Turned away from what is right or good: Corrupt. b. improper, incorrect. c. contrary to the evidence or the direction of the judge on a point of law perverse verdict. Behavior that deviates from that which is understood to be orthodox or normal. Definition of Sorcery: The Use of power gained from the assistance of controlling spirits outside of the authority of God*

1Ki 16:31 And it came to pass, as if it had been a light thing for him to walk in the sins of Jeroboam the son of Nebat, **that he (Ahab) took to wife Jezebel the daughter of Ethbaal king of the Zidonians, and went and served Baal, and worshipped him.** *32 And he reared up an altar for Baal in the house of Baal, which he had built in Samaria. 33 And Ahab made a grove; and Ahab did more to provoke the LORD God of Israel to anger than all the kings of Israel that were before him.*

Rev 2:18 And unto the angel of the church in Thyatira write; These things saith the Son of God, who hath his eyes like unto a flame of fire, and his feet are like fine brass; 19 I know thy works, and charity, and service, and faith, and thy patience, and thy works; and the last to be more than the first. 20 **Notwithstanding I have a few things against thee, because thou suffers that woman Jezebel, which calleth herself a prophetess, to teach and to seduce my servants to commit fornication, and to eat things sacrificed unto idols. 21 And I gave her space to repent of her fornication; and she repented not.**

Notice the admonition, message and word given to the church of Thyatira. *I know your deeds, your love and faith, your service and perseverance* and that they had grown from where they began in the beginning. But they tolerated another message. They tolerated the teaching of another teacher that was not teaching the values or vision given to them by God through the Angel of the Church. As a result, the Angel of the church was being rebuked, because there was immorality within the church. What was the source of the immorality? Was it Jezebel? On the surface it just appears to be the teaching of Jezebel that was the source of immorality, but this was not directly the source of the immorality. The source of the immorality was, firstly the toleration of mixture. The church had mixture with the vision or message of the church from the Angel (Pastor), and the Message of the woman Jezebel that called herself a prophetess. Secondly, the disorderly relationship with the Angel of the Church and the teacher that's called Jezebel. Notice she hadn't been ordained or recognized as a prophetess in the church by the Angel of Thyatira, but she called herself a prophetess. She was a self-proclaimed prophetess. Therefore, the Lord, in Revelation 2:19, called her, *"that woman Jezebel, THAT CALLS HERSELF A PROPHETESS (Someone who hears from God for the people),* But she was outside of the leadership and message given to the Angel of the church.

Thirdly, the source of the immorality was that the woman that called herself a prophetess, was being allowed to teach and lead those following her astray. The source of the immorality was the teaching that was not in line with the values or the vision of the church, from the angel of the church. It was not necessarily that she was teaching them to commit immorality, but that her teaching that was not in line with the teaching of the angel of the church of Thyatira, was releasing a spirit of immorality into those that were being influenced by her leadership.

But I have this against you, that you tolerate the woman Jezebel, who calls herself a prophetess, and she teaches and leads My bondservants astray SO THAT they commit acts of immorality. The teaching wasn't necessarily immoral, but it led to immorality because it was not in line with what was originally given by the Angel of the Church. Therefore, I have this against YOU (Angel). The Angel of the church was being rebuked, because He was tolerating Jezebel. It's not a light thing for God to resist you and have something against you. Therefore, the Jezebel spirit begins with another message, other than the message that was originally given by God, a message coming outside of the authority of God, or outside of the authority over a nation, household, people, or organization.

The SPIRIT of Jezebel was in the Garden with Adam & Eve

The spirit of Jezebel didn't begin with the Old Testament Jezebel, but all the way back in the garden with the serpent tempting the human race through the deception of Eve to receive another message or directive that God never gave mankind, in order to seduce them to partake of the tree of the knowledge of good and evil.

Gen 3:1. Now the serpent was craftier than any other beast of the field that the LORD God had made. He said to the woman, "Did God actually say, 'You shall not eat of any tree in the garden'?"

The Spirit of Jezebel wants to cause you to receive another message other than the message that has been given by God-ordained authority. This is what the serpent did to Eve. He deceived Eve by putting doubt in her mind about what God had said. And because God had not spoken directly to Eve, but to Adam, he was able to present to her doubt about the tree of the knowledge of good AND evil. Notice the tree was both good AND evil. The evil was shrouded over and covered with good works, deeds and words. God had not spoken to Eve directly and because of that I believe that's why the serpent went to Eve and not Adam. *Gen 2:16 <u>And the LORD God commanded the man, saying,</u> Of every tree of the garden thou* *mayest freely eat: 17 But of the tree of the knowledge of good and evil, thou shalt not eat of it: for in the day that you eat thereof thou shalt surely die.*

The Spirit of Jezebel will attempt to get to the one who has not had an encounter with God or who is not submitted correctly with the one who has had an encounter with God, to attempt to deceive and place doubt in their spirit about what God has said, just as the serpent did to Eve....*Hath God Really Said*... Gen 3:1

How do we overcome the Spirit of Jezebel?

We must submit to God ordained authority so that we can encounter God for ourselves, to receive the message of the Lord. *(I Cor. 15:4-5)*

....4. and that He was buried, and that He was raised on the third day according to the Scriptures, and that He appeared to Cephas, then to the twelve.

After that He appeared to more than five hundred brethren at one time, most of whom remain until now, but some have fallen asleep;

then He appeared to James, then to all the apostles; and last of all, as to one untimely born, He appeared to me also. **1 Cor. 15:4-8 NASB**

Remember from the Introduction, no Apostolic voice in scripture went with the message of the gospel until they first submitted to God ordained authority (*The man Christ Jesus for 3- and one-half years*) in order that they may encounter the resurrected Glorified Christ (*GOD HIMSELF after His resurrection in the mountain in Galilee*).

He Appeared to Them

God sent His son as a Man (Jesus) to connect us with God. Once we are submitted to God-ordained authority (a man or woman of God), we can encounter the Glorified Christ (God) for ourselves.

<u>Once we are connected to the right message through right positioning with God-ordained authority, to encounter God for ourselves, we can overcome the temptation of the evil one to chase another message that gets us out of our place in the Kingdom.</u> We must find the God-ordained authority God is leading us to submit to, and then go after an encounter with God for ourselves, to be kept from the evil one.

Being Delivered from Jezebel

To be delivered from the seduction of Jezebel's seductive teachings we must confess Jesus AS LORD, and we must know the Authority or Angel (Pastor) God has placed in our lives to disciple us into His will and purpose for our lives, and we must do John 8:31 AND CONTINUE IN HIS WORD AS DISCIPLES (Disciplined ones)...So Jesus was saying to those Jews who had believed Him, "If you continue in My word, then you are truly disciples of Mine; and you will know the truth, and the truth will make you free. "John 8:31-32 (NASB)

Ro. 10:9 that if you confess with your mouth Jesus as Lord and believe in your heart that God raised Him from the dead, you will be saved; for with the heart a person believes, resulting in righteousness, and with the mouth he confesses, resulting in salvation.

Knowing who the authority (covering) is in your life and confessing the commands (word) of that authority in your life to get it in your heart and then guarding your heart from any other message, is the key to deliverance from the Evil One (JEZEBEL).

The Seven-Fold Process to Deliverance

Joel 2:32 And it shall come to pass, that whosoever shall call on the name of the LORD shall be delivered: for in mount Zion and in Jerusalem - shall be deliverance, as the LORD hath said, and in the remnant whom the LORD shall call.

Luke 4:18 The Spirit of the Lord is upon me, because he hath anointed me to preach the gospel to the poor; he hath sent me to heal the brokenhearted, to preach deliverance to the captives, and recovering of sight to the blind, to set at liberty them that are bruised, 19 To preach the acceptable year of the Lord.

These verses of scripture in Luke 4:18, 19 and Joel 2:32, along with any others the Holy Ghost highlights as you're praying in tongues, should especially be declared each 6th day, *(as well as any day you feel the need),* in order to emphasize and impart into your heart the vision, mission and purpose of Christ to encounter our hearts for deliverance. And in order to make sure that you catch the spirit of deliverance in your own spirit, to go forth to do what Christs' vision directs those that call on the Name of the Lord, and who the spirit of the Lord rest upon.

Luke 4:18, 19, was the mission statement that Jesus quoted right after he came out of His wilderness temptations. This mission statement was YESHUA'S LIFE calling, what it consisted of and who He was. When we meditate on, and quote these verses, we are signifying that we are coming out of our wilderness temptations, being delivered from Jezebel, this religious, political and economic world system of Darkness. It signifies we are coming out of debt, distress, and discontentment, coming into YESHUA'S LIFE, to preach in the power of the spirit, releasing His fame to go forth throughout the region, the nation, and the world.

Calling on The Name of The Lord for Deliverance - *Joel 2:32 And it shall come to pass, that whosoever shall call on the name of the LORD shall be delivered: for in mount Zion and in Jerusalem shall be deliverance, as the LORD hath said, and in the remnant whom the LORD shall call.*

To call on the name of the Lord is the Hebrew word **QARA - QâRâ' kaw-raw'** *A primitive root (rather identical with H7122 through the idea of accosting a person met); 1. to call out to (that is, properly address by name, but used in a wide variety of applications): - bewray [self], that are bidden, call (for, forth, self, upon), cry (unto), (be) famous, guest, invite, mention, (give) name, preach, (make) proclaim (-ation), pronounce, publish, read, renowned, say.*

<u>**Qara**</u> - *means to call out to, to address by name, to be famous, to invite, to preach, to pronounce, to read, to publish, to proclaim.*

In order to be delivered you have to call on the name of the Lord. Most people think that calling on the name of the Lord is just calling on Yeshua like we call our friend across the street, or how we call our loved one on the phone, calling their name out to get their attention. But calling on the name of the Lord is more than that.

The Hebrew word for *"Call"* above, lists seven things that calling on the name of Lord entails. When you include these seven things within the framework of your seeking the Lord you will get Yeshua to manifest in the midst of your life to bring deliverance. And as we continue in these seven things as a part of daily/weekly devotions, it causes us to walk in the delivered life. The seven points of calling on the Name of the Lord are:

The Seven Points of Calling on the Name of the Lord

1. Read about him – *(Read something)*
2. Address Him by name – *(Know something-the name of the Lord)*

3. Call out to Him – *(Say something – confess Him w/your mouth)*
4. Invite him in – *(Ask something - for him to be your messiah)*
5 Make him Famous – *(Exalt Him – that name above every name)*
6. Write about him – *(Journal something)*
7. Preach about him – *(Proclaim something)*

The reason why we don't get delivered or if we get the delivered, the reason we don't stay delivered is because we don't call on the name of the Lord in the Hebrew sense of the word, to call. We stop at confessing; we stop at inviting him into our life. However, calling on the Name of the Lord entails reading about Him, studying and knowing His name, who Yeshua is, calling out to Him, asking him to be your earthly messiah, ruling and reigning your life in every aspect of your life, exalting him above every circumstance, problem, addiction or any person or thing in the earth. It entails writing about him in journals, diaries, and books, and then preaching and proclaiming him to a lost and dying world. To walk in the Delivered Life, we have to really call on the name of the LORD.

<u>Pray this at least once OUT LOUD</u>: Heavenly Father, I ask you to forgive me of all sins I have committed against you and against those made in your image. Lord I ask that Your spirit surround myself and my family members and protect us according to your word in Psa. 34:7. I now declare Isaiah 54:17 "No weapon formed against me and my family members shall prosper in the mighty Name of Jesus Christ, Yeshua Ha Mashiach. Amen.

NOW PRAY IN TONGUES UNTIL YOU'RE BUILT UP ON YOUR MOST HOLY FAITH IN THE WORD OF GOD YOU'VE BEEN MEDITATING ON TODAY. Jud 1:20 But ye, beloved, building up yourselves on your most holy faith, praying in the Holy Ghost,

Pray this OUT LOUD: *In the Name of Jesus Christ. I sever all demonic spirits from any demonic ruler above these demonic spirits. I revoke any orders given to any of these demonic spirits and demonic forces concerning me and my family. I bind all demonic entities under the one and highest authority I loose you, evil spirits, from us now. I loose you to where Jesus Christ sends you. Your assignments and influences in our lives are broken now! IN THE NAME OF THE LORD JESUS CHRIST, AMEN!*

<u>PRAY IN THE SPIRIT</u>: PRAY IN TONGUES UNTIL YOU'RE BUILT UP ON YOUR MOST HOLY FAITH IN THE WORD OF GOD YOU'VE BEEN MEDITATING ON TODAY. *Jud 1:20 But ye, beloved, building up yourselves on your most holy faith, praying in the Holy Ghost,*

In the Name of Jesus Christ, I declare broken and destroyed all spell, hexes, vexes, curses, voodoo practices, witchcraft, occult, masonic and satanic rituals, masonic and satanic blood covenants, masonic and satanic blood sacrifices, demonic activities, evil wishes, covenant rituals, all occult, Islamic and coven fasting prayers and curse-like judgments that have been sent out way and have been passed down through my family generational bloodline. I loose them to where Jesus Christ sends them. I ask forgiveness for, and renounce all negative inner vows made by myself. I ask you Lord Jesus Christ that you release us from these vows and from any bondage they may have held us in. Lord in the name of Jesus Christ, do not remember the iniquities of our forefathers against us (Psalm 79:8)

NOW PRAY IN TONGUES UNTIL YOU'RE BUILT UP ON YOUR MOST HOLY FAITH IN THE WORD OF GOD YOU'VE BEEN MEDITATING ON TODAY. *Jud 1:20 But ye, beloved, building up yourselves on your most holy faith, praying in the Holy Ghost.*

PRAY THIS OUT LOUD: In the Name of the LORD JESUS CHRIST, according to Hebrews 4:12, I take the Sword of the Spirit, which is the Word of God, and cut myself and my family members free from all generational. Inherited sins, weaknesses, character defects, personality traits, cellular disorders, genetic disorders, learned negative inner vows, and spiritual and psychological ties. I cut all bonds that are not of the Lord and put the Blood of Jesus Christ between us. I cut all bonds of the relationships of each one of us that are not of the Lord, back to the beginning of time and all present and future generations. By the Sword of the Spirit. And in the Name of Jesus Christ, I say that we are cut free, and we are free indeed. We are now free to become the children of God as the Lord intended us to be.

CHAPTER 12

(Day 7) FOR YOURS IS THE KINGDOM THE POWER AND THE GLORY

The Worship Anointing

(Saturday Day 7) - Today Pray in tongues for at least 30 minutes and meditate on I Chr. 29:11-13 Malachi 1:11, along with this 7th phrase from the Disciples Prayer: <u>Yours is the Kingdom the Power and the Glory</u>

TODAY'S MEDITATION: The final dimension in the Disciples prayer is the Heavenly Realm of the Worship Dimension in prayer, accessing the greatness of the Kingdom of God, "For yours is the Kingdom, the Power and the Glory forever, Amen.

The Connection of Jesus' High Priestly Prayer with the Disciples Prayer

This phrase of the *Disciples Prayer* "<u>Yours is the kingdom the Power and the Glory</u> "connects with Jesus' high priestly prayer in verse 24, *Father, I will that they also, who you have given me, be with me where I am;* **that they may see my glory**. To understand the 7th phrase of the Disciples prayer we must understand the genesis of this prayer. This prayer that was given to the disciples by Jesus did not originate with Jesus. Most New Testament believers don't readily realize that Jesus came to fulfill the Old Testament. What that means is that He was the Old Testament revealed.

The Old Testament, or the first testament is the New Testament concealed and the New Testament is the Old, or First testament revealed. Therefore, when the Apostles wrote in the New Testament, they were explaining the mysteries or revelation behind the scriptures of the Old. When Jesus taught, he was revealing what the Old had been concealing. Even the Prayer that He taught His disciples did not originate with him, but with David when he was dedicating Solomon's Temple in 1 Chronicles 29:1-22. It was this prayer the Jesus taught His disciples to pray that would cause His people to usher in the final glory and power of the Temple of the Messiah which would be His body or House in the earth.

The Phrase *YOURS IS THE KINGDOM, POWER AND GLORY* is taken from David in 1 Chronicles 29 after David and His rulers had offered up to God an exceeding Great offering to dedicate and consecrate the temple of Solomon. After this offering David blesses the people and says this prayer.

1Ch 29:11 Thine, O LORD, is the greatness, and the power, and the glory, and the victory, and the majesty: for all that is in the heaven and in the earth is thine; thine is the kingdom, O LORD, and thou art exalted as head above all.

1Ch 29:12 Both riches and honor come of thee, and you reign over all; and in thine hand is power and might; and in thine hand it is to make great, and to give strength unto all.

1Ch 29:13 Now therefore, our God, we thank thee, and praise thy glorious name. Jesus, giving His disciples this prayer to pray was telling them that their faithfulness to pray this prayer as a corporate people, would make them the family of God, with Him being their father. It would also make them the House or Temple of God, with Him being their High Priest, and would make their lives a pleasing offering to God with Him receiving the offering of their hearts as a pure sacrifice, releasing fire on the altar for the nations to see the greatness and power of His people, His house and their King and His Kingdom.

This prayer reveals how the Kingdom of God will come in power and great glory....Through a revelation of God as Father, Son and Holy Ghost, through His people looking to him for their daily bread, receiving forgiveness of their sins by the sacrifice of His Son, and forgiving one another as an offering of a sweet smelling savor, walking in purity in the kingdom of God, free from the deception of the evil one. His people would be a pure offering unto the Lord as David and His rulers offered to God in 1 Chron. 29, resulting in what Malachi says, in 1:11

From the rising of the sun to the setting of the same, My, name will be great among the nations, and in every place, incense is going to be offered to My name and a grain offering that is pure, for My name will be great among the nations, says the Lord of Hosts.

This picture in this 7th phrase of the *Disciples Prayer* "Yours is the Kingdom Power and Glory" is also found in John's Revelation of Jesus Christ, in Revelation 4:10,11;

Rev. 4:10, 11 the four and twenty elders around the throne lay down their crowns at the feet of Jesus, the lamb on the throne.

At this final level and phrase of the *Disciples Prayer* we are placing at the feet of Jesus, our Messiah, our crowns as we worship Him that sits on the throne. We are enthroning Him King of the earth as He sits on the throne in Jerusalem, upon His return to the earth as King of king and Lord of Lords, seated upon David's Throne.

The Ultimate picture and sacrifice of Worship is actually offering back to God what He gave to us, in order that He may accomplish His will through us, and not us accomplishing our will through Him. This is seen in Genesis 22:14 As Abraham gives back to the Lord the promised seed, Isaac on Mount Moriah.

Gen 22:1 *And it came to pass after these things, that God did tempt Abraham, and said unto him, Abraham: and he said, Behold, here I am.*

2 And he said, Take now thy son, thine only son Isaac, whom you love, and get thee into the land of Moriah; and offer him there for a burnt offering upon one of the mountains which I will tell thee of.

3 And Abraham rose up early in the morning, and saddled his ass, and took two of his young men with him, and Isaac his son, and clave the wood for the burnt offering, and rose up, and went unto the place of which God had told him.

4 Then on the third day Abraham lifted up his eyes, and saw the place afar off. 5 **And Abraham said unto his young men, Abide ye here with the ass; and I and the lad will go yonder and <u>worship,</u> and come again to you**.

6 And Abraham took the wood of the burnt offering, and laid it upon Isaac his son; and he took the fire in his hand, and a knife; and they went both of them together.

7 And Isaac spake unto Abraham his father, and said, My father: and he said, Here am I, my son. And he said, Behold the fire and the wood: but where is the lamb for a burnt offering?

8 And Abraham said, My son, God will provide himself a lamb for a burnt offering: so they went both of them together.

Most believers never enter into this final realm of worship because it's difficult to give back to God what we know has been given to us by God. But true worship is offering back to God what He's given to us, to declare it was yours in the first place and it all came from you, and we offer it back to you as worship to you.

1Ch 29:12 **Both riches and honor come of thee, and you reign over all; and in your hand is power and might; and in your hand it is to make great, and to give strength unto all.** *13 Now therefore, our God, we thank you, and praise thy glorious name. 14 But who am I, and what is my people, that we should be able to offer so willingly after this sort?* **for all things come of thee, and of thine own have we given thee.**

When we enter into this worship dimension in the earth, we will hasten the return of the Lord. He can't come until we worship Him back, declaring this earth belongs to Him, He gave it to the sons of men (Psa. 115:116), and as rulers in the earth, we must take our place of authority to declare it belongs to Him, and invite Him to take His place on the throne of our hearts and ultimately on the throne in Jerusalem, Israel in the earth.

TODAY'S INDIVDUAL PRAYER DECLARATION *I declare today that yours is the kingdom, the power and the glory forever. I declare that all I have has come from you, and it belongs to you. I declare that all you've given me; I give it back to you. I declare that you sit on the throne of my heart as king of kings and lord of lords. And I invite and invoke you to sit on the throne of my life as king over all I have and all I am. Come lord Jesus and take your place as ruler over the whole earth. I announce that your kingdom is an everlasting kingdom and your glory will be forever and ever. Receive my crown today as worship. I place it at your feet. I place my calling, and giftings at your feet. I place my talent and abilities at your feet. I place my businesses at your feet. I place my ministry at your feet. It was yours before it was mine, and i give it all back* *to you. Receive it as worship today. Receive it as my sacrifice of praise today, and let incense arise from the rising of the sun to the going down of the same, in all the earth forever, and ever in Jesus name, amen.*

(Saturday Day 7) - **Today Pray in tongues for 30 minutes and meditate on First Chronicles 29:10-18; Malachi 1:1-11 Matthew 23:37-39; Revelation 4:10; Revelation 22:17, along with this 7th phrase from the Disciples Prayer: FOR YOURS IS THE KINGDOM THE POWER AND THE GLORY FOREVER, AMEN!**

Scriptural Meditation for Yours is the Kingdom the Power & Glory

1Ch 29:10 Wherefore David blessed the LORD before all the congregation: and David said, Blessed be thou, LORD God of Israel our father, for ever and ever.

1Ch 29:11 Thine, O LORD, is the greatness, and the power, and the glory, and the victory, and the majesty: for all that is in the heaven and in the earth is thine; thine is the kingdom, O LORD, and thou art exalted as head above all.

1Ch 29:12 Both riches and honour come of thee, and thou reignest over all; and in thine hand is power and might; and in thine hand it is to make great, and to give strength unto all.

1Ch 29:13 Now therefore, our God, we thank thee, and praise thy glorious name.

1Ch 29:14 But who am I, and what is my people, that we should be able to offer so willingly after this sort? for all things come of thee, and of thine own have we given thee.

1Ch 29:15 For we are strangers before thee, and sojourners, as were all our fathers: our days on the earth are as a shadow, and there is none abiding.

1Ch 29:16 O LORD our God, all this store that we have prepared to build thee an house for thine holy name cometh of thine hand, and is all thine own.

1Ch 29:17 I know also, my God, that you try the heart, and hast pleasure in uprightness. As for me, in the uprightness of mine heart I have willingly offered all these things: and now have I seen with joy thy people, which are present here, to offer willingly unto thee.

1Ch 29:18 O LORD God of Abraham, Isaac, and of Israel, our fathers, keep this forever in the imagination of the thoughts of the heart of thy people, and prepare their heart unto thee:

1Ch 29:19 And give unto Solomon my son a perfect heart, to keep thy commandments, thy testimonies, and thy statutes, and to do all these things, and to build the palace, for the which I have made provision.

1Ch 29:20 And David said to all the congregation, Now bless the LORD your God. And all the congregation blessed the LORD God of their fathers, and bowed down their heads, and worshipped the LORD, and the king.

1Ch 29:21 And they sacrificed sacrifices unto the LORD, and offered burnt offerings unto the LORD, on the morrow after that day, even a thousand bullocks, a thousand rams, and a thousand lambs, with their drink offerings, and sacrifices in abundance for all Israel:

Mat 23:39 For I say unto you, Ye shall not see me henceforth, till ye shall say, Blessed is he that cometh in the name of the Lord.

Rev 4:10 The four and twenty elders fall down before him that sat on the throne, and worship him that lives for ever and ever, and cast their crowns before the throne, saying, 11 Thou art worthy, O Lord, to receive glory and honor and power:

Rev 22:17 And the Spirit and the bride say, Come. And let him that heareth say, Come.

TODAY'S CORPORATE PRAYER DECLARATION: *We declare today that yours is the kingdom, the power and the glory forever today. We declare that all we have has come from you, and it belongs to you. We declare that all you've given us; we give it back to you. We declare that you sit on the throne of our heart as King of Kings and Lord of Lords. And we invite and invoke you to sit on the throne in Jerusalem as king over all the earth. Come lord Jesus and take your place as ruler over the whole earth. We announce that your kingdom is an everlasting kingdom and your glory will be forever and ever. Receive our crowns today as worship. We place them at your feet. We place our calling, and giftings at your feet. We place our talents and abilities at your feet. We place our businesses at your feet. We place our ministries at your feet. They were yours before they were ours, and we give it all back to you. Receive it as worship today. Receive our sacrifice of praise today, and let incense arise from the rising of the sun to the going down of the same, in all the earth, forever, and ever in Jesus name, amen.*

P A R T 3

MAKE US ONE – JOHN 17 UNITY & CITY FATHERS

CHAPTER 13

THE PROCESS TO JOHN 17 UNITY

Joh 17:22 And the glory which thou gave me I have given them; that they may be one, even as we are one:

Joh 13:3 Jesus knowing that the Father had given all things into his hands, and that he was come from God, and went to God; 4 <u>He arose from supper and laid aside his garments; and took a towel and girded himself. 5 After that he poured water into a basin, and began to wash the disciples' feet, and to wipe them with the towel wherewith he was girded</u>. John 13 - 17

With John 17 being primarily overlooked and the least emphasized of all the biblical prayers in scripture, it's probably why we've overlooked the mystery for the process to coming into John 17 unity that's found in these chapters leading up to this prayer, beginning in John 13 (The Last supper/Shabbat/Feast of Passover

Seder). Within these chapters, all of which are recorded in red, is the process to John 17 Unity.

Practical Steps to Answering Jesus' Prayer That We Would Be One.

The Process of the Lords Supper/Shabbat in the Feasts of the Lord are actually the process of a family becoming one and Awakening to the beauty of who they are in Christ, by connecting with their God-given Covenant and blessing. John 13 is the initiation of the process of the Lord's Prayer in John 17 that they would be ONE. Many read the prayer of Jesus in John 17, that we would be one, and think that the prayer begins in John 17, but it actually begins in John 13, with Jesus washing His disciple's feet, and telling them that He's about to leave them, and go to the cross, but that He would not leave them without a comforter but would send the Holy Spirit to be in them.

Again, as we noted earlier, the Holy Spirit is given as the function of how we would answer Jesus' Prayer for us to be one. The Holy Spirit is given that the body would be ONE. John 13 is the initiation of this process of the Lord's Prayer in John 17 that they would be ONE after He left. Jesus wanted the love of father to be in them, so they could love one another with His love, not the love of the world. Jesus began this process in John 13, by having a Shabbat meal where he gathered his disciples to initiate the process of becoming ONE. The process beginning in John 13 thru John 17 reveals 12 expressions of ministering one to another that if initiated within the body, unity and oneness would be the natural result. I call these 12 practical steps to unity, the 12 ONE ANOTHERS OF UNITY. These 12 expressions of ministering one to another, that Jesus modeled for His disciples, beginning with washing their feet, are as follows:

The 12 One Another's Of Unity

1. Foot washing - SERVE ONE ANOTHER. Joh 13:13 - nip'-to - To cleanse (especially the hands or the feet or the face); ceremonially to perform ablution: - wash. Compare G3068.-

Joh 13:13 Ye call me Master and Lord: and ye say well; for so I am. 14 If I then, your Lord and Master, have washed your feet; <u>ye also ought to wash one another's feet.</u>

Php 2:1 If there be therefore any consolation in Christ, if any comfort of love, if any fellowship of the Spirit, if any bowels and mercies, <u>2 Fulfil ye my joy, that ye be likeminded, having the same love, being of one accord, of one mind.</u> 3 Let nothing be done through strife or vainglory; but in lowliness of mind let each esteem other better than themselves. 4 Look not every man on his own things, but every man also on the things of others. <u>5 Let this mind be in you, which was also in Christ Jesus: 6 Who, being in the form of God, thought it not robbery to be equal with God: 7 But made himself of no reputation, and took upon him the form of a servant, and was made in the likeness of men: 8 And being found in fashion as a man, he humbled himself, and became obedient unto death, even the death of the cross.</u>

9 Wherefore God also hath highly exalted him and given him a name which is above every name: 10 That at the name of Jesus every knee should bow, of things in heaven, and things in earth, and things under the earth; 11 And that every tongue should confess that Jesus Christ is Lord, to the glory of God the Father.

2. Receiving a New Commandment to Love- LOVE ONE ANOTHER. John 13:34, 35

Joh 13:34 A new commandment I give unto you, that ye love one another; <u>as I have loved you, that ye also love one another</u>.

3. Don't Be Troubled believe in God believe also in ME - BELIEVE IN ONE ANOTHER. Joh 14:1

Joh 14:1 Let not your heart be troubled: ye believe in God, <u>believe also in me.</u>

4. I Go to prepare a place for you that where I am there you may be also. - MAKE ROOM FOR ONE ANOTHER. John 14:2

Joh 14:2 In my Father's house are many mansions: if it were not so, I would have told you. <u>I go to prepare a place for you.</u>

5. If you had KNOWN ME, you would know the father- KNOW ONE ANOTHER- John 14:7

Joh 14:7 <u>If ye had known me,</u> ye should have known my Father also: and from henceforth ye know him and have seen him.

To word "know" in this passage, if you had known me, you should have known my father gives the connotation that knowing man is connected to a knowledge of God. Jesus connects them knowing Him, the son of man/son of God with knowing God the father. This knowing is not a theological knowledge, nor is it a head knowledge, but this knowing of one another is a knowing that is connected a word in the Greek that has implications of a type of knowledge that comes from dwelling with one another as a Husband does his wife, or as a family member knows one another. It's an intimate knowing that a husband is to have towards his wife.

6. The WORD that I Say unto You...- SPEAK THE WORD TO ONE ANOTHER. Jn 14:10

Joh 14:10 Believe thou not that I am in the Father, and the Father in me? <u>the words that I speak unto you</u> I speak not of myself: but the Father that dwelleth in me, he doeth the works.

7. Greater Works Shall You Do - WORK WITH ONE ANOTHER. Jn 14:12

Joh 14:12 Verily, verily, I say unto you, He that believeth on me, <u>the works that I do shall he do also</u>; and greater works than these shall he do; because I go unto my Father.

8. Ask (Pray) and the Father will send you the comforter - PRAY FOR ONE ANOTHER. Jn 14:16

Joh 14:16 <u>And I will pray the Father, and he shall give you</u> another Comforter, that he may abide with you forever;

9. Abide in me and I in you - ABIDE WITH ONE ANOTHER. Jn 15:1,2,4

Joh 15:1 I am the true vine, and my Father is the husbandman. 2 Every branch in me that bears not fruit he taketh away: and every branch that bears fruit, he purges it, that it may bring forth more fruit. 4 <u>Abide in me, and I in you. As the branch</u>

cannot bear fruit of itself, except it abide in the vine; no more can ye, except ye abide in me.

10. You are my Friends if you do what I command you (to love one another) - BE-FRIEND ONE ANOTHER - Jn 15:14

Joh 15:14 Ye are my friends, if ye do whatsoever I command you. 15 Henceforth I call you not servants; for the servant knows not what his lord doeth: but I have called you friends; for all things that I have heard of my Father I have made known unto you.

11. When the Helper comes, He will guide you into all truth - HELP ONE ANOTHER - Jn 15:26

Joh 15:26 But when the Comforter is come, whom I will send unto you from the Father, even the Spirit of truth, which proceed from the Father, he shall testify of me:

12. Weep and Lament and be turned to joy - WEEP AND REJOICE WITH ONE ANOTHER- John 16:13

Joh 16:20 Verily, verily, I say unto you, that ye shall weep and lament, but the world shall rejoice and ye shall be sorrowful, but your sorrow shall be turned into joy.

These 12 expressions of ministering one to another, that Jesus revealed to His disciples right before He prayed in John 17, for them to be one, are vitally connected to His prayer. Without these twelve practical expressions of ministry and connection one to another, that Jesus modeled and communicated to His disciples, His prayer for them to be one is devoid of the power to produce this oneness. This prayer doesn't begin with this first verse in John 17, it begins with the prelude to the prayer, with Jesus' final address to His disciples in John 13. If leaders in the body of Christ today would meditate on these chapters to be able to portray and relay these ministry virtues to their followers, and then memorize the main 4 points of emphasis of John 17, then the disciple's prayer of Matthew 6 would automatically release kingdom power and glory, when we come together to pray, for one another, with one another. In the remaining pages of this chapter you will learn the 4 main points of emphasis of Jesus' prayer in John 17, that will help the church leader memorize and meditate on the focus and perspective of Jesus, that enabled Him to pray with passion and purpose for the unity and oneness of His followers. This purpose and passion in prayer will release the commanded blessing into regions in the earth where this prayer is prayed, and its virtues modeled. There are 4 perspectives of unity that Jesus covers in His prayer that will empower leaders to attain to the spirit of Christ to unite leaders and followers alike around a greater glory than temporal, earthly success and notoriety in our individual ministries.

The Eternal Perspective for Unity

There is a strange anomaly that exists between Christ and His church, which probably has something to do with why we've rarely ever arrived at John 17 unity in our communities of faith in regions or in cities within the body of Christ in the earth. Everybody's striving for glory here in the earth. Everybody's striving for position here in the earth. Everybody's striving for recognition here in the earth. And everybody seems to be striving for success as is measured by earthly measurements here in the earth. But Jesus seemed to be more focused on an eternal perspective and the glory than he was to receive as he was reunited with the father in the Godhead and leaving this planet to be reunited and restored to that glory in heaven with the father. There seems to be a fourfold process to John 17 Unity that is rooted in an Eternal Perspective to ministry that temporal perspective ministries (Ministries looking for glory here in the earth) often minimize, overlook or misprioritize. As a result, we are separated, segregated and divided from one another as we go after a more temporal, success motivated assignment that focuses on grandeur and praise in the eyes of men. However, within this eternal perspective there seems to be an obvious process to achieving the Unity of John 17. The process is;

The Assignment Perspective (v.2-10) *Accomplishing the work the Father has given Him in the earth, to give eternal life, to manifest the father's name to the men He gave Him, to give them the words the father has given to Him.*

The Eternal Life Perspective (v.13-22) *An acknowledgment that we are not of this world, we are living for another life, and this life is an internship for that life. An acknowledgment of the need to be sanctified from this world by the truth of the word of God. An acknowledgment of the need to be kept in the world from the evil one, not taken out of the world. An acknowledgment of the need to be one with the father, and with one another to be kept in this world and from the evil one.*

The Glory Perspective (v.22-24) *To see Christ in His glorified state in order to receive the glory of the father and be with Him where He is. This prayer of the glory of the father that Jesus desired them to see was seen by John, the recorder of this John 17 prayer of Jesus, in the book of the Revelation of Jesus Christ. John saw Jesus in all of His glory as He revealed His plan to transition the earth to the age to come, and the Kingdom's of this world become the Kingdoms of our God and His Christ (anointed ones).*

The Love Perspective (25, 26) – *That the Knowledge of the Father's love for mankind and His love plan to send His only son to die for the sins of Humanity would be known to mankind and that we would have partake of the Love of the father, and to know Love the father has for the Son is the same Love the father has for each one* *of us.* What was the glory that he had before the world began? What was the position He fulfilled in the Godhead before the world began? What was it that Jesus was being reconciled and restored to in heaven that he considered more glorious than anything He did or could ever do on the earth? To ascertain the answers to those questions we must ask ourselves, "What is that Jesus is doing in heaven right now as we speak?" Whatever He's doing right now in heaven, this is the glory he had before the world began. So, what is he doing right now as we speak in heaven? Hebrews 7 and Romans 8 gives us glimpse into what he considered the glory He had before the world began.

Heb_7:25 Wherefore he is able also to save them to the uttermost that come unto God by him, seeing he ever lives to make intercession for them.

Rom_8:34 Who is he that condemns? It is Christ that died, yea rather, that is risen again, who is even at the right hand of God, who also makes intercession for us.

Jesus was, from the beginning, and forever is, an intercessor, taking the words from the heart of the father and speaking them into existence in the earth. This is Jesus' highest calling, over every earthly calling he fulfilled while on the earth. There are many functions of ministry that Jesus undertook while on the earth. He operated as an Apostle, he operated as a Prophet, as a Pastor, he operated as a Teacher and as an Evangelist. However, of all those ministry offices the greatest ministry function that Jesus operated in while in the earth, and the ministry office that he still functions in while seated at the right hand of the father, is the ministry office of a High Priest, after the order of Melchizedek.

This is the eternal calling of every believer in the earth and the glory we had in HIM, before the world began. When we begin to focus on this eternal glory and calling from the eternal perspective, and take this high priestly prayer that Jesus prayed and begin to meditate on it, and pray it like we do the Disciples Prayer in Matthew 6, I believe we will begin to see Him in all of His glory, like John did in the book of the Revelation of Jesus Christ, and we will enter into a dimension of His expression of communities of faith like we've yet to tap into here in the earth. We need an understanding of our eternal calling and mission in eternity as priests after the order of Melchizedek, in order to avoid the pitfalls to John 17 unity that are placed before us by the spirit of this age here in the earth. We need an eternal perspective to be established in an eternal principle of the Unity of the Spirit (Eph 5:2, 3).

Eternity was the focus of Jesus' ministry here while he was in the earth, putting eternal life into the hearts of men, and eternity was what was on his mind as he was preparing to leave the earth. Jesus only measured his success by whether or not he gave eternal life to as many as the father had given him. His focus was not on the number the father had given, but the quality of life that he imparted into those whom the father had given him. This focus on eternal life, an eternal perspective he defines as knowing the father, the only true God, and Jesus Christ who the father had sent. This is what He defined as eternal life. This is what he measured as having accomplished the will and work of the father in the earth - *that he should give eternal life to as many as the father has given him.* This eternal perspective – knowing God the Father, and the Son, and being reconnected with the eternal glory of God – is what is missing from Christ's disciples in the Church in the generation at the end of the age. This revelation is what we need to have restored to our generation in order to attain unto John 17 Unity.

CHAPTER 14

THE REVELATION OF JESUS CHRIST –

The Glory Encounter Needed for John 17 Unity

As I began to meditate more and more on the first 3 or 4 verses of John 17, I began to get a thirst and hunger for a truer and more complete revelation of eternity, along with a greater desire to know God. As I did, I began to see something about the Apostle John and the prayer that Jesus prayed in John's book, in chapter 17. I began to see the key to understanding what it takes to attain unto this type of unity. The third perspective to the process to John 17 Unity entails getting a revelation of Jesus as the glory of God, or the glorified Christ. The Apostle John, the writer of this book had actually received Jesus' hope and prayer for John's life, detailed in another book that John had written – *The book of the Revelation of Jesus Christ*. One of the main and major points of emphasis that Jesus prayed for his disciples in this glory perspective in verse 24 was that they would see His glory: *Father, I desire that they also, whom you have given me, may be with me where I am, to see my glory that you have given me because you loved me before the foundation of the world.*

Jesus wanted them to see him in his glory. John, having wrote the book of John, caught a hold of that desire from this prayer of Jesus, and positioned himself to see the glorified Christ detailed in his other book about this revelation, called the Revelation of Jesus Christ. As I realized that this was the process to John 17 unity, I felt impressed to add the book of the Revelation to my prayer time during these days of worship and prayer and contending for John 17 unity in my city. And as I did the spirit of God said these words to me; "<u>The key to the city Church coming together in unity in any region in the earth is found in the Revelation of Jesus Christ.</u>"

As I heard these words, I was prompted to challenge these words, by going to the book of the Revelation, in the back of my bible, to begin reading from verse 1, looking for keys to how Pastors and Church fathers could work together in any region in the earth to build a City Church as one unified body. I must confess I was skeptical about finding these keys to regional unity in the body of Christ in a region in the book of the revelation, because I had read this book many times before I had never had anything like that jump out at me. But this morning I got up off my knees and I began to read the book of the revelation of Jesus Christ. **The revelation of Jesus Christ, which God gave him to show to his servants the things that must soon take place. He made it known by sending his angel to his servant John, who bore witness to the word of God and to the testimony of Jesus Christ, even to all that he saw. Blessed is the one who reads aloud the words of this prophecy, and blessed are those who hear, and who keep what is written in it, for the time is near. John to the seven churches that are in Asia: Grace to you and peace from him who is and who was and who is to come, and from the seven spirits who are before his throne, and from Jesus Christ the faithful witness, the firstborn of the dead, and the ruler of kings on earth. To him who loves us and has freed us from our sins by his blood and made us a kingdom of kings and priests.**

As soon as I began reading the first 8 verses of the book of the revelation, immediately I began to get 8 clear steps to coming into John 17 unity from His revelation. Remember the Book of the revelation of Jesus Christ was written by the same author, John the beloved. The same author that was the only one of the synoptic gospels to record Jesus' high priestly prayer to be returned to His former glory, and to have that glory revealed to His disciples, is the author that records what he saw when Jesus' prayer is answered, and His glory is revealed to John on the isle of Patmos. As I began reading this revelation of Jesus' glory revealed to John, I began to realize what Jesus was saying concerning giving eternal life to His disciples, that they would know the only true God and Jesus Christ who He had sent. Jesus was saying and revealing in John 17 that the purpose and reason He had been giving authority over all flesh was to release to humanity the eternal nature and knowledge of the glory of God in Jesus Christ. I refuse to believe that this is a coincidence. I refuse to believe that it is a coincidence that John recorded this prayer in John 17, and John is the primary author that saw the glorified Christ. The first step from the book of Revelation, to John 17 unity is a revelation of Jesus eternal glory.

The following are the 8 steps to coming into John 17 unity from the book of the Revelation.

1. A Revelation of Jesus Christ. v.1 - What is the revelation of Jesus Christ that must be stamped upon our hearts? The revelation of His death, burial and Resurrection. We must get a revelation of how he lived, how he died, and how God raised him from the dead, so that we might live, die, and be raised up to sit in heavenly places in HIM. (Philippians 2:2-11)

Complete my joy by being of the same mind, having the same love, being in full accord and of one mind. Do nothing from selfish ambition or conceit, but in humility count others more significant

than yourselves. Let each of you look not only to his own interests, but also to the interests of others. Have this mind among yourselves, which is yours in Christ Jesus, who, though he was in the form of God, did not count equality with God a thing to be grasped, but emptied himself, by taking the form of a servant, being born in the likeness of men. And being found in human form, he humbled himself by becoming obedient to the point of death, even death on a cross.

2. A Revelation of the things to come in the End Times v.1

...to shew unto his servants' things which must shortly come to pass; John said, I was in the spirit on the Lord's Day...I was there at the end of the age on the Lord's Day of vengeance, the great and terrible day of the Lord, in the spirit. And was given a mandate to right what he had seen. This revelation that he was given began with Jesus Christ in his glorified state, the Church in Revelations 2 and 3 without spot or wrinkle, and then the Day of the Lord, the bowl, seal and trumpet Judgments sent upon the earth through the praying Church, both in heaven and in the earth. The Church that gets a revelation of her purpose at the end of the age will come together as one in his house of prayer for ALL nations.

3. A Revelation of the Angelic assignments of the Churches in a region v.1, 11-15.

....and he sent and signified it by his angel unto his servant John: Each church in every region has a prophetic assignment to fulfill for the word over that region to come to pass. Each church has an Angel that is assigned to that body in the region to release progressive revelation of the heart of God and the prophetic words over that region. Once we know our assignment in the region and keep our candle lit, the body in the region can become a force. In Asia there were seven churches representing the seven golden candlesticks that John saw Jesus standing in the midst of. Every

major region has at least seven major expressions with seven major assignments to light and shine forth in that region. **In the place of regional corporate prayer, we find our assignment within the assignments of the whole region.**

Rev 1:10 I was in the Spirit on the Lord's day, and heard behind me a great voice, as of a trumpet, 11 saying, I am Alpha and Omega, the first and the last: and, What thou seest, write in a book, and send it unto the seven churches which are in Asia; unto Ephesus, and unto Smyrna, and unto Pergamos, and unto Thyatira, and unto Sardis, and unto Philadelphia, and unto Laodicea.

4. A Revelation of the call to the Great commission witnessing of the Word of God and the Testimony of Jesus Christ to all in a region.v.2

Who bare record of the word of God, and of the testimony of Jesus Christ, and of all things that he saw. John 17 Unity requires getting a corporate world vision for the salvation of the regions in the earth we are assigned to. Jesus said, **go ye into all the earth and preach the gospel to all nations** (Matt 28:19). In order to go into all world and preach to all nations, you must have a place of prayer in the House of Prayer for all nations (Isaiah 56:8). And you must get a revelation of the word of God for that region and the testimony of Jesus in that region. We must get a revelation of the regional, city harvest that God wants to release for whole cities to be saved, and then we must answer the call to the great commission in our region.

5. A Revelation and keeping of the Prophetic words (Prophecies) over a region and the Blessing that is released in keeping those prophecies v.3

Blessed is he that reads, and they that hear the words of this prophecy, and keep those things which are written therein: for the time is at hand. Every region has a prophetic word that has been revealed and spoken over that region. When we tap into the prophetic word over the region we have been called to, there is a blessing to comes upon the church, community of faith that taps into that word, speaks and preaches that word, and reads it aloud.

6. A Revelation of the Grace and Peace from the Seven Spirits of God around the throne. (Keeping the lamps lit) v.4

Rev 1:4 John to the seven churches which are in Asia: Grace be unto you, and peace, from him which is, and which was, and which is to come; and from the seven Spirits which are before his throne; For John 17 Unity there must be a revelation of the **grace and peace that comes upon the corporate body of Christ that lights the lamps of prayer and the word (prophetic assignment) over their region before the throne of God.** Seven spirits around the throne of God corresponds to the seven churches, purposes for fulfillment in a region. We come before throne of God, the place of corporate prayer in the regional house of prayer or city church there is a grace and peace that comes upon the church in the region to fulfill their particular assignment in that region.

7. A Revelation of the Priesthood ministry of the Kingdom of God v 6; John 17:1 Hebrews 5, 6 (Melchizedek Priesthood of Jesus Christ).

Rev 1:5 And from Jesus Christ, who is the faithful witness, and the first begotten of the dead, and the prince of the kings of the earth. Unto him that loved us and washed us from our sins in his blood.

In order for there to be John 17 unity, the body of Christ must go from the first principles of the doctrine of Christ in Hebrews 6:1-6 to the Forerunner ministry of Jesus Christ after the order of

Melchizedek (Hebrews 6:19). This is the priesthood ministry that every believer is being perfected for by the five-fold ministry gifts in the body, to bring (pray) reconciliation of God to man, man to man, and heaven to earth, for the return of Christ to set up his kingdom in the earth (2 Cor. 5:17-21). We are called to be priests after the order of Melchizedek, to pray; THY KINGDOM COME THY WILL BE DONE, IN EARTH AS IT IS IN HEAVEN. The Unity of the faith begins with the perfecting, (maturing) of the body of Christ for their priesthood ministry of intercessory reconciliation of God/heaven to earth. It's the understanding of the corporate King/Priest ministry of the believer after the order of Melchizedek to re-possess the earth for Christ and His kingdom, that we break the spirit of division, competition and strife in the church as related to ministries, ministry gifts etc. The highest office in the body is the priest hood ministry of the believer after the order of Melchizedek. The Apostle/Prophets etc. are the foundation, that when the house is built, is the unseen part of the building.

8. A Revelation of the coming of the Lord v.7

Rev 1:7 Behold, he cometh with clouds; and every eye shall see him, and they also which pierced him: and all kindreds of the earth shall wail because of him. Even so, Amen.

An End-time Corporate Prayer Transition

There's a transition happening in the earth and it involves the proclamation and prayers of believers that will call heaven to earth. As we move closer to the end of the age understanding the 7 phrases from the *Disciples Prayer* that will precipitate divine encounters with Christ, to hasten His return in the earth will become more and more pronounced as the Church becomes a House of Prayer for all nations. We are in the midst of this transition in prayer. This transition is being seen right before our eyes. Yet many are not aware of it.

This generation has replaced prayer with theological training in school, studying concepts and the theological and ideological basis for what they believe about eschatology, or the study of the end-times or the study of Christ. But too often we don't pray and encounter the Christ in the Theology we're studying about. Theology is actually the study of God. The way we should be studying God, in addition to training and study in His word, is by encountering Him in prayer. The Lord is calling for more than knowledge, He's calling for an encounter with Him that will release us into a great co-mission that will usher back into the earth, Jesus the Christ. As you now know, the great commission is not about preaching the gospel, but about making disciples of the kind of encounter prayer that His disciples received in the mountain of God in Galilee. This great commission didn't begin in Matthew 28:19 with going into the world....it began in Matthew 28:10,16 with a directive to meet Him in the mountain to see the glorified Christ.....**Before you Go Ye, Go See** through praying and saying the 7 phrases of the *Disciples Prayer*.

DECLARATION OVER THE GREATER COLUMBUS REGION:

Father we declare Columbus will be saved *and it will be a city where the Lord's shalom (peace and wholeness) is present according to Isaiah 65:17-25.*

WE DECLARE THAT...

1. *Our city will be a city where there is joy. (v.18)*

2. *Our city will be a city where there is the absence of weeping and crying (v.19)*

3. *Our city will be a city where there is no infant mortality*

neither within or without the womb.

4. *Our city will advance our neighborhoods in all ethnicities, races and cultures in this city.*

5. *The races of our city will be united and work in unity and harmony.*

6. *Our city will be a city where its inhabitants live out their full lives (v.20)*

7. *Our city will be a city where people build houses and live in them. (vv. 21, 22)*

8. *Our city will engage and promote strong, distinct, and vibrant neighborhoods.*

9. *Our city will be a city where there is fulfilling and meaningful work (vv.22)*

10. *Our city will provide an atmosphere that promotes job creation and economic growth in existing and emerging industries.*

11. *Our city will be a city where there is confidence that the next generation will face a better life.*

12. *Our city will be a city where people experience the blessing of God (.23)*

13. *Our city will be a city where there is intergenerational family support with family structure intact*

14. Our City will be a city where there are rapid answers to prayer. (v.24)

15. Our city will be a city where there's an absence of violence (v.25)

16. We declare that Columbus is a **good city**, a **strong city**, and a **city of Refuge**

DECLARATION OVER THE CHURCH/BODY OF CHRIST IN GREATER COLUMBUS:

Father we declare that the Body of Christ in Greater Columbus will be BLESSED and walk in our full inheritance according to the prayer of Jesus in John 17

WE DECLARE THAT…

1. We shall be Kept in His name. (v.11)

2. We Shall be one with one another, as He is one with the Father.

3. We shall have HIS Joy made full in us by the words he spoke while He was in the world (The 4 gospels). (v8)

4. We shall be kept in the world. (v15)

5. We shall be kept from the Evil one. (v15)

6. *We shall be sanctified through the truth (revelation) of the Word (v17).*

7. *We shall be ONE with our forefathers in the faith (both past & present) as well as one with Jesus. (v21).*

8. *We shall be perfected (matured) in oneness (unity). (v22)*

9. *We shall be with Him where He is. (v23)*

10. *We shall see His glory. (v24).*

11. *The Love that the Father Loved the Son with will be in us. (v26)*

12. *Jesus (the Son) will be in us. (v26).*

……IN JESUS NAME

OTHER BOOKS BY BRONDON MATHIS ON AMAZON.COM

Religion Racism & Reconciliation – *A Message from God's Word to African-American Christians about Injustice Forgiveness and Reparations* -

Out of the Trayvon Martin shooting, the Ferguson, Missouri, Michael Brown shooting, as well as the New York City, Eric Garner death, a dormant volcanic racial divide has erupted, that has been hidden beneath the surface of the American society for decades, leading to riots, protests, and the tragic assassinations of two NYC policemen.

In this book RELIGION RACISM AND RECONCILIATION Brondon Mathis explains how African-American Christians can draw on their faith to deal with social, judicial and economic injustice and come to a place of healing, forgiveness and racial reconciliation, unlocking the keys to reparations and restoration of the lost years of oppression and racial injustice. He shares his experiences, testimonies and revelation of how God delivered him from racial bitterness and unforgiveness, by the Word of God, from the hurtful past in America of Slavery, the racial oppression of Jim Crow laws and legislated racial discrimination, taking him from a bitter life to a better life.

Religion Racism and Reconciliation would benefit everyone, Christian, and non-Christian alike, Black, or White, Jew, or Gentile, that wishes to see Dr. Martin Luther King Jr's dream of Reconciliation become a reality - *Clyde Morris Pastor, Pennsylvania.*

List Price: $14.99

The 12 Dimensions of the Heart of God - **12 Steps to Becoming a Person or Church after God's Own Heart** –

As we move further into the second decade of the 21st century there's a sense that the second coming of Christ is nigh at hand. As His appearing nears the Spirit of God is prompting men and women in prayer rooms and houses of prayer all over the world to go from seeking God for material things and shallow spiritual experiences to seeking, like David, after One Thing - The Beauty of God's Heart - To behold the beauty of the Lord. In this book Brondon Mathis gives revelation on the 12 dimensions of what's on God's Beautiful Heart for His church and His people at the end of the age, to raise up a people who will fulfill all of the will of God for their generation. It describes each characteristic of God's heart in detail and will take the reader on a 12-step journey from their own heart to God's own Heart.

List Price: $14.99

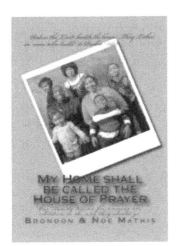

My Home shall be called the house of Prayer - Our Family Vision for training our children in the way they should go.

List Price: $14.99

The Church without Spot or Wrinkle 7 steps to Becoming A Pure & Spotless Bride Ready For the Day of the Lord -

The Church without Spot or Wrinkle reveals how the end-time Church will be prepared as a bride adorned for her husband, right before the coming Day of the Lord, by taking heed to the messages given to the seven churches of Asia in the book of the Revelation.

List Price: $14.99

My House shall be called the House of Prayer. The 7 Principles to becoming a Praying Church -

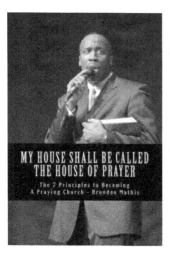

Mat 21:13-16 And He said unto them, (It is written), My house shall be called the house of prayer (for all nations); but ye have made it a den of thieves. From these verses in Matthew 21:12-18 there are 7 principles, all of them beginning with a "P" that will return the end-time church back to her calling as the house of prayer. This book is aimed at exploring these 7 principles for the purpose of restoring joyful prayer back to the church of the 21st century, to enable her to fulfill her end-time mission in the earth of preparing the way for the coming of the Lord

List Price: $14.99

The Coming FORERUNNER Ministry Out of AFRICA - Africa & African America's End-Time Calling bringing Gods house of Prayer to Reconciliation and Fullness -

At the end of the age God is releasing His spirit to prophetically call forth a unique group of end-time forerunners out of Africa & the African Diaspora to arise, shine with light in the time of gross darkness, to take their place of leadership in the earth, to stand shoulder to shoulder with the nations of the world to lead the church to reconciliation and fullness

List Price: $14.99

The Melchizedek Priesthood of Jesus Christ -*The 7 Steps to The Priesthood of The Believer in God's House of Prayer* -

There are many functions of ministry that Jesus undertook while on the earth. He operated as an Apostle, he operated as a Prophet, as a Pastor, he operated as a Teacher and as an Evangelists. However, of all those ministry offices the greatest ministry function that Jesus operated in while in the earth, and the ministry that he still functions in while seated at the right hand of the father, is the ministry office of a High Priest, after the order of Melchizedek. He is an intercessor, ever living to make intercession for His people to be reconciled to God. This ministry of reconciliation from the priesthood of Melchizedek is the main ministry that Jesus came to fulfill. **List Price: $14.99**

My Money is Restored - Preparing to Arise During The Coming Financial Fall Out -

All indicators say our economic system in America and the world is headed for a complete financial collapse. If we act now to free ourselves from this debtor system and learn how to operate with godly wisdom and discipline with our resources, we will not only survive this coming economic disaster, we will ARISE AND THRIVE and see the long-awaited transfer of the wealth of the nations into the hands of the righteous. "MY MONEY IS RESTORED" will explore the life of the biblical personality Joseph in Egypt, along with His principles for money restoration, and unconventional strategies for accumulating wealth during down economic times in the world's financial markets. My Money is Restored is aimed at empowering believers to operate within the world's financial markets, through unconventional wisdom, by the system and principles of the Kingdom of God, to establish wealth and financial abundance during times of lack, for the preservation and glorification of the Church in the earth. **List Price: $14.99**

Upon This Rock I will Build My Church -The End-Time Purpose of the Church built upon the book of the revelation

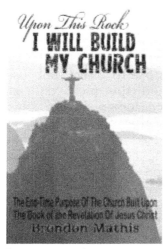

From Matt 16:13-17 this book will explore the Rock that the church was built upon to position her to accomplish her end-time purpose in the earth. From these verses we can see clearly what the rock is. #1 The Church was built upon the Revelation of Jesus Christ - Thou art the Christ, the Son of the Living God. #2 The Church was built for battle - the gates of hell will not prevail against it. #3 The Church was built upon Prayer, to bind the kingdom of darkness, and to release heaven on earth - and whatever you bind on earth shall be bound in heaven... whatever you loose on earth will be loosed in heaven. To accomplish her mission the church must understand the person revealed in the book of the Revelation of Jesus Christ. Only the church built upon this rock will be able to withstand the gates of Hell at the end of the age, to prepare the earth for Jesus' return.

List Price: $14.99

Building Cities of Refuge – **Preparing cities through 24/7 Worship & Prayer for the Coming Systemic Collapse –**

"Building Cities of Refuge" is a book on how certain cities will be positioned during the unique dynamics surrounding a coming systemic collapse to thrive, not just survive, during the most difficult times in all of Human History. This book reveals that by as early as 2015, because of this coming systemic collapse, the Church in our nation is going to need to develop relational networking communities and regions of economic and agricultural supply for our livelihood, to be able to survive, as well as thrive during these times. These communities will be called CITIES OF REFUGE & POCKETS OF MERCY. God is moving on believers in these designated Cities of Refuge, all over the nation and world, to begin building City Churches for 24/7 day and night worship and prayer, along with storehouses for storing food in these communities; places where people can come and receive spiritual and natural food and essentials for living during this coming systemic collapse. This book will present some of these solutions and scriptural paradigms for cities of refuge, as well as wisdom and principles for living for the Church during this time.

List Price: $14.99

The Beginning of Sorrows – *Biblical Paradigms for the comfort and peace of Jerusalem in Times of Conflict*

As the Peace talks between Israel and the Palestinian Authority continue to produce little results, and while a nuclear Iran becomes a reality right before our eyes, Jerusalem is coming upon a season that Jesus prophesied about in Matthew 24:8 called the Beginning of Sorrows. What should be our response to this season of conflict and impending war in Jerusalem and the Middle-East? Where should believers in Christ stand on the issue of Jerusalem and how should we pray? In this book, the Beginning of Sorrows, Brondon Mathis shares from a divine encounter he had in the city of Jerusalem, which unlocked for him the biblical text of Matthew 24, that is meant to position Jerusalem to be prepared for this season of sorrow, as well as for the return of her Messiah, who will ultimately bring an end and peace to this ancient biblical conflict.

List Price: $14.99

In the Beginning of Sorrows, you will learn:
1. What really is the Peace of Jerusalem?
2. What one sign from Matthew 24 will initiate the Beginning of Sorrows in Jerusalem?
3. How will God comfort Jerusalem with His rod and staff?
4. What are the coming Judgments of the Four Blood Moons?
5. What is the gospel that must be preached before the end to this conflict comes?
6. How do we correctly pray for the Peace of Jerusalem?
7. How will All Israel be saved from the desolation of this Holy City?

Contact info:
Brondon Mathis
614 425-7427, office
614-745-9683, cell
yeshuamovement@gmail.com
www.brondonmathis.com
facebook/brondonmathis.com